香港手語課程(高級)

HONG KONG SIGN LANGUAGE (ADVANCED)

香港聾人福利促進會
The Hong Kong Society for the Deaf

第一版 2007年 7月
第二版 2009年 3月
第三版 2011年 7月
第四版 2014年 1月
第五版 2019年 1月

First published July 2007
Second published March 2009
Third published July 2011
Fourth published January 2014
Fifth published January 2019

國際標準書號 ISBN: 978-962-7334-16-2

示範：林國福小姐、湯敏珊小姐
翻譯：黃寶翔先生
編輯：陳玉娟小姐、黎穎思小姐、蕭慧欣小姐

Demonstrators : Miss Lam Kwok-fook Angel, Miss Tong Man-shan
Translator : Mr. Wong Po-cheung James
Editors : Miss Chan Yuk-kuen, Miss Lai Wing-sze,
Miss Siu Wai-yan Rebecca

目　　錄

CONTENTS

序

我跟香港聾人福利促進會的接觸始於我對手語的研究。當時有一組由Ursula Bellugi教授帶領的美國學者邀請我一起探討各類手語的型格性質，因此我需要學習香港手語，並且搜集香港手語的構造特徵。我加入聾福的手語班，也閱讀過現有課程的課本。從這些精心設計的材料中，我學到香港手語中獨特的手形、位置和動作。後來我更把學到的手語單詞用廣東話的語法連貫起來跟聾人交談。這時我覺得自己能「用」手語了，加上我在聾福遇上的每位聾人會員都很包容，使我這個信念變得更強。我天真地以為會做每個手語字詞就等如會「說」手語。直至做了一點研究之後，我才瞭解自己過往的手語表達，只是字對字的 「硬譯」而已。

創造語言是人類一項獨特的天賦。健聽的人利用語音組成語言的單位去做句子；失去聽力的人則利用視覺。跟其他語言一樣，手語是一個獨立的語言，有它自己的特徵、形態和文法。跟凸字不同的是：手語並非建基於口語。通過研習美國手語（ASL），我發現手語其實是由不同層次的語言單位組成，透過特定的語法，基層的單位與高層次的單位，又和更高層次的語言單位連結來表達意思。香港手語的基層構成單位仍有待發現。我們開始注意到有些香港手語的手形和指節間的移動是美國手語中沒有的，也許這就是兩個語言之間一項重要的分別。

這套手語書幫助我們對香港手語有基礎的認識。當中的影像光碟使我們可以記錄香港手語的現有內容，更可以反映我們在初、中、高各程度所使用的教學材料。有別於其他手語書，這套材料除了強調個別字詞外，更向學員示範它們應用在連貫的「交談」中如何改變。更值得一提的是：在這本高級教材中，編者嘗試更進一步向學員揭示現實生活中聾人溝通時的動作。只有通過真實的生活體驗，我們才會真正學到語文，做到活學活用。

霍陳婉媛博士
二零零七年六月二十二日
香港大學

Foreword

My first contact with the Hong Kong Society for the Deaf was through my research on sign language. Being invited by the American team, led by Professor Ursula Bellugi, to work on the formal properties of sign languages, I had to acquaint myself with the sign language in Hong Kong and what it was that made it so special to gain the status of a separate language. I joined classes organized by the Society and went through some of the materials presented in the present course book. Through the carefully designed items, I learned the special hand configurations, hand orientations and movements that were unique to Hong Kong Sign Language. Later on, I also learned to combine the individual signs to form sentences following the ways I converse in Chinese. At that time, I felt that I was 'speaking' the language and sure enough the signers I met in the Society were so kind as to reinforce this belief of mine. I was so naïve to think that to be able to sign was to be able to remember how to sign each vocabulary item. It was not until I had done some research that I realized that I was then only communicating through word-to-word translation.

To be able to conceive a language is a special endowment of the human race. Those who can hear, make use of speech sounds to form units and those who are deprived of the ability of hearing, make use of their vision. Sign language is an autonomy language like any other human languages with its unique distinctive features, morphology and grammar. Unlike braille, it is not a system based on the spoken language. Through the study of American Sign Language (ASL), I have learned that there were layers of visual units that were combined into the next layer of larger units by means of rules and regulations. What exactly are the basic units in Hong Kong Sign Language still remain to be discovered. Actually we are beginning to note that there are a lot of hand internal movements in Hong Kong Signs that are not present in ASL and this may point to one important area of distinction between the two languages.

The present series of sign books helps us to lay the foundation to further understanding of Hong Kong Signs. Its DVD collection helps us to document what is already there. It also forms a record of the materials we use in our beginners, intermediate and advanced courses. Unlike other sign books, the materials presented do not only put emphasis on individual signs but also show the learners how they are being modified in continuous 'speech'. It is also worth noting that in this advanced book, the writers venture a lot more into what the signers do in actual communication. It is only through genuine life situations that we get to learn how real languages are being used.

Angela Fok
22 June 2007
The University of Hong Kong

前　　言

從《香港手語課程（中級）》到《香港手語課程（高級）》出版相隔差不多一年，我們謹向本會中級課程的畢業同學致歉，並感謝他們就教材提出寶貴意見，有助於本書的編制。

本會的手語中心自70年代開始舉辦手語訓練班，教授社會人士運用手語溝通，手語中心由2005年起整理訓練班的教材，編成一系列的「香港手語課程(初級、中級及高級)」，協助學員在參與課堂互動式的教授之餘，更能準確掌握課堂內容；而新課程亦能對有興趣研習香港手語的人士作參考資料。初級課程讓學員認識運用手語的基本技巧，引發學習興趣；中級課程為有志繼續學習手語的人士提供更多不同範疇的詞彙、對話訓練；而高級課程則適合欲深入了解手語的人士，提供更深更廣的詞彙、多種形式的練習，以豐富運用手語的能力。

汲取了編寫初級和中級教材的經驗，本書增添了多項練習，讓同學能自行在家練習，希望更充分地利用視像光碟（DVD）的優點，來加強各位的理解能力，提高學習效果。部分練習的資料來自中文報章和網頁，因此，手語影片所提供的是原文的手語翻譯版本。語言翻譯是沒有標準答案的，本書的影片示範僅是一個可供參考的演繹方法，希望藉此讓同學對如何將中文翻譯成香港手語有初步的認識。

本書承蒙　霍陳婉媛博士撰寫引言，謹此致以萬二分謝意。同時亦要向曾經提供協助的多位人士致以摯誠的謝意，包括林國福小姐、湯敏珊小姐、何國彪先生及盧瑞華小姐就手語方面作出建議，還有義務英文翻譯黃寶翔先生，以及繪畫插圖的周家欣小姐。

最後，由於時間倉促，加上經驗所限，本書內容難免有不足之處，懇請各界人士賜教。

總幹事
黃何潔玉
二零零七年五月

Preface

First of all, we would like to apologize for the late publication of this book. It has been a year since the publication of 'Hong Kong Sign Language (Intermediate)'. We would also like to thank the students of our intermediate courses. Their opinions help a lot in compiling this book.

The Sign Language Centre of the Society has been organizing sign language classes for the public since 70s. In 2005, the Centre re-edited the training course material, and reorganized it into a series of training course-books, "Hong Kong Sign Language (Elementary, Intermediate and Advanced level)". In addition to the interactive learning in classroom, learners can better benefit from the newly edited books for they provide more accurate and detailed illustration. Moreover, the course-books can serve as reference for those who are interested in learning Hong Kong Sign Language. The elementary-level course was written to help learners to grasp the basics of Hong Kong Sign Language and simulate their interest in further studies. The intermediate-level course aims at strengthening learner's ability with wider spectrum of glossary and conversational exercise. For those who would like to study Hong Kong Sign Language on a long-term basis, the advanced-level course offers a more extensive spectrum of glossary and various exercises to sharpen their skills.

In order to make full use of the advantage of the visual property of DVD for learning enhancement, various exercises are provided for self-learning at home. The articles in the exercises have been selected from various newspapers and websites with the original text in Chinese. Hence, the videos shown in DVD are the sign language translation of the original scripts. There is no model answer when it comes to language translation. The signing shown in the DVD is just one of the possible versions of translation for the learners' reference. We hope it would give the learners an initial understanding of how translation can be done from Chinese into Hong Kong Sign Language.

We are deeply grateful to Dr. Angela Fok for writing the preface for this book. Special acknowledgement goes to Miss Lam Kwok-fuk Angel, Miss Tong Man-shan, Mr. Ho Kwok-biu and Miss Lo Sui-wah for their valuable advice on sign language. We would also like to extend our warmest thanks to Mr. Wong Po-cheung James for preparing the English translation, and Miss Vanessa Chau for the illustrations.

Lastly, due to limited time and lack of experience, the contents of this book might contain imperfections. Any feedback will be highly appreciated.

Director
Wong Ho Kit-yuk, Winnie
May 2007

使用說明

1. 手語慣用語

・列舉的五個常見手語慣用語中，除解釋其意思外，每個手語都附有應用例子，先講解應用時的情況，再按手語句法寫成例句／簡短對話，應用例子示範可參考DVD。（影片只提供手語字幕）

2. 字詞

・某些字詞會加入下列指示，以協助學員掌握正確的動作。

・由兩個或以上的手語組合而成的複合手語，以*表示，如：世界杯* ＝ 世界＋舉起獎杯。

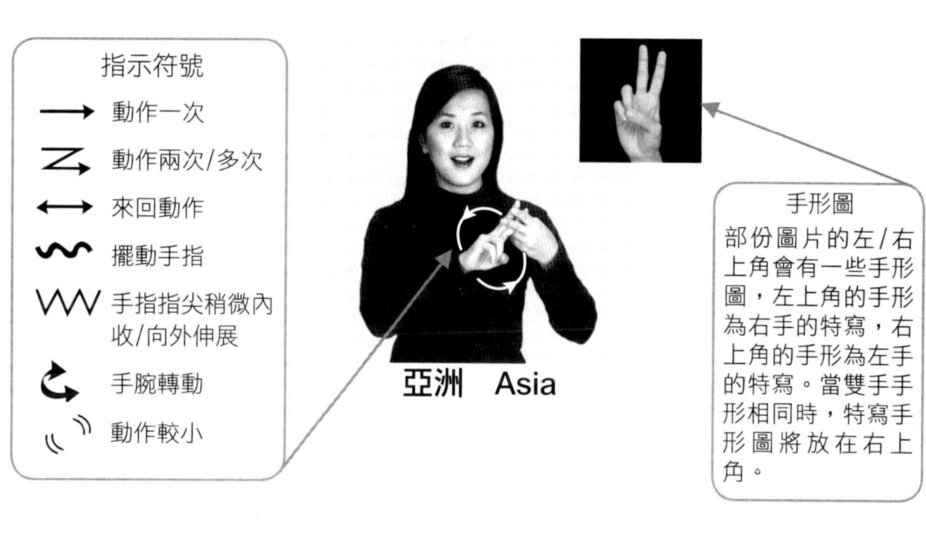

3. 課後練習

・第一至八課的字詞後，分別有不同形式的練習，包括對話、選擇題、短文及觀看理解，學員須觀看DVD進行練習。練習後學員可自行參閱練習答案，另附上部分影片原稿以供參考。

User's Guide

1. Idiomatic Signs

- For the five common idiomatic signs listed, apart from explaining their meaning, each sign is shown with an example application plus a description on the context and a sentence/simple dialogue in signing sequence. For a demonstration of the examples, please view the DVD. (the footage subtitle only shows the signs)

2. Words

- In order to help learners to acquire the correct movements, some words may include the following instructions:
- Compound signs that are expressed by the combination of two or more signs will be marked with *, for example: World Cup* = world + raising the trophy cup

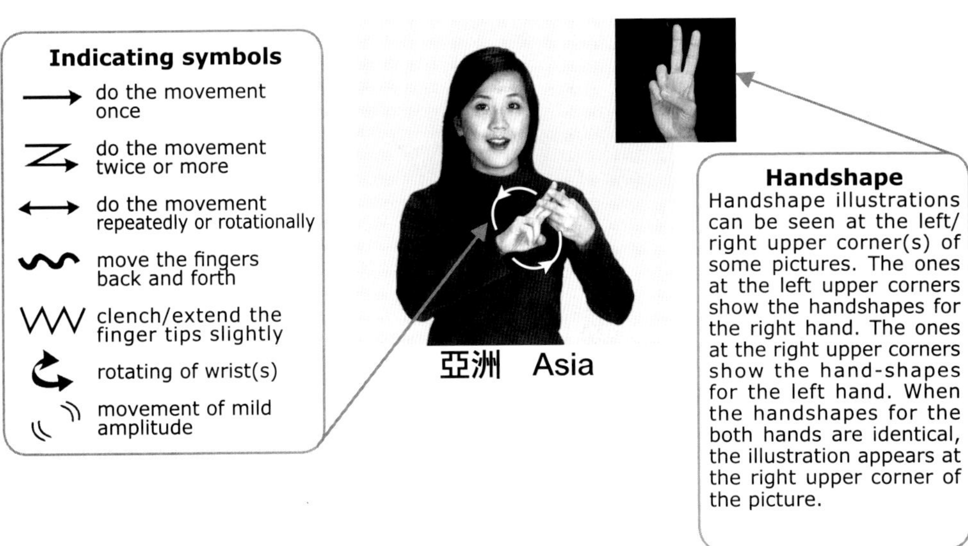

3. Exercise after each Chapter

- In chapter one to eight after the glossary section, there are exercises in different formats including dialogue, multiple-choice questions, essays and comprehension. Learners have to watch the DVD so as to do the practice. After doing the exercises, the learners can check the suggested answer themselves and refer to the scripts of the part of the footages.

手語慣用語

跟其他語言一樣，手語也會有一些富特色的慣用語。這些慣用語有特定的用法及意思，有時很難用另一種語言的詞彙來翻譯它們的意思，就像廣東話和英語，有些香港人慣用的廣東話，是很難用英語把原有的意思表達出來。故此，在運用這些慣用語時便要小心，而且要多花時間觀察和請教聾人，才能熟練地在日常對話中應用出來。如你能巧妙地運用手語慣用語，聾人便會對你另眼相看，就像一個外籍人士，能操地道的廣東話一樣，令你感到驚喜和佩服。

以下有五個常見的手語慣用語簡介和應用例子，希望藉此加深你對它們的了解。

手語慣用語 1

用於事物或活動時，有最喜歡、喜愛、愛好的意思。〔參考第一課對話一〕

例一：雞翼／我／～～，／飯／扒飯多次／3／可以。

用於人時，則表示好朋友、老友。

例二：我倆／一起長大／～～。

手語慣用語 2

形容當事情已經發生了，不能重頭再來，或回復事情未發生前的一樣，有已成定局、已發生的不能改變、米已成炊等意思。〔參考第一課對話二〕

例：甲和乙計畫跟團去旅行，甲原以為向公司請假不會有問題，便和乙一起報團及繳交了訂金。豈料甲的申請不獲公司批准，甲唯有告訴乙，並問可否退回訂金。乙便會用這個手語回答，表示已成定局、不能改變等意思。

甲：我／請假／不能，／旅行團／錢／退／可以？
乙：不能！／～～。

手語慣用語 3

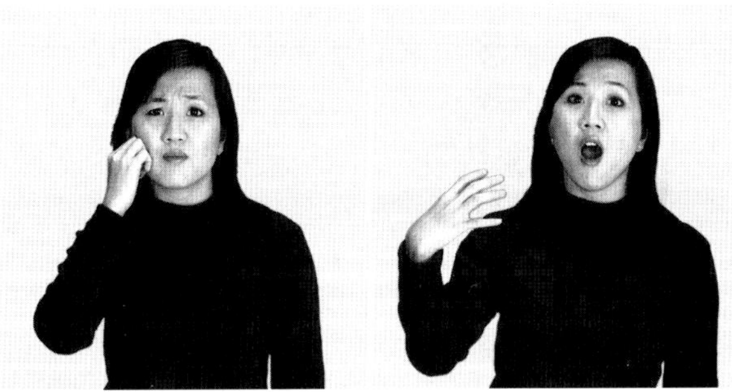

當有意想不到、意料之外、爆冷門等情況／事件出現時，聾人便會打出這個手語。〔參考第一課對話二〕

例：昨天是一年一度的聾人乒乓球比賽，甲告訴乙昨天的賽果後，乙感到很意外。

甲：昨天／乒乓球／<手語名>／勝利。
乙：～～！／<手語名>／乒乓球／很差。

手語慣用語4

這是一個頗常用的慣用語，表示繼續不變，保持原狀，有照舊、依舊、仍然的意思。〔參考第二課對話二〕

例：甲和乙是老朋友，大家很久沒見，見面便閒談近況。甲問乙是否仍然住在旺角，乙回答依舊是住在那裡，沒有變。

甲：你／家／旺角？／你？／～～？
乙：對！／我／～～。

手語慣用語5

當看到另一人表達的想法，和自己所想或正想「說」出來的一樣時，聾人便會打出這個手語，有不約而同、恰巧你想的和我想的一樣、想法一致等意思。

例：甲和丙談論有關兩位聾人朋友已結婚的事，丙不認同甲，於是甲便向乙求証，証明乙和自己的想法一致後，便會做出這個手語。

甲：<手語名>／<手語名>，／結婚／完了？
乙：對！／秘密／結婚／完了！
甲：～～（一手在乙的前面，一手在自己前面）

Idiomatic Signs

Like any other language, Hong Kong Sign Language has its unique idioms. As these idioms have their own specific usage and meaning, sometimes it is quite difficult to express them in another language. The case is similar to what is happening between Cantonese and English, there are occasions when a colloquial Cantonese expression fails to find its counterpart in the English language. So, we have to be careful when using these idioms. A word of advice would be to spend more time in observing the signing of Deaf people and to ask them if necessary, so as to familiarize yourself with the application of idiomatic signs in daily conversations. When you have acquired appropriateness and spontaneity in deploying idiomatic signs, the Deaf people will view you differently, showing surprise and a special respect, just like how you would feel when you meet a foreigner who can speak fluent colloquial Cantonese.

Below is a brief introduction of five common idiomatic signs, which we hope could enhance your understanding of the subject.

Idiomatic sign 1

When used to describe an item or activity, it means 'favourite'. [refer to dialogue 1 in chapter 1]

Example 1: chicken wings/I/~~,/rice/motion of taking in rice/3/can.

When used to describe persons, it means 'best friend' or 'close friend'.

Example 2 : we two/grow up together/~~.

Idiomatic sign 2

It is used to express the meaning 'what has been done cannot be undone' or 'there is no alternative but to accept what has already happened.' [refer to dialogue 2 in chapter 1]

Example: A and B had intended to go on a tour. At first, A thought there would not be a problem in getting leave from his employer, so he joined a tour together with B and handed in the deposit. Unexpectedly A's leave application was rejected by his employer. A could do nothing but to relate the news to B. He also asked if the deposit could be refunded. B would reply him using this sign, expressing the meaning that what has been done cannot be undone.

A : I/apply leave/cannot,/tour/money/return/can?
B : cannot!/~~.

Idiomatic sign 3

When something surprising, unexpected or least possible happens, the Deaf people will use this sign [refer to dialogue 2 in chapter 1]

Example: It was the annual ping-pong competition for the Deaf yesterday. After A told B of yesterday's result, B felt very surprised.

A : yesterday/ping-pong/<name sign>/win.
B : ~~!/<name sign>/ping-pong/very poor.

Idiomatic sign 4

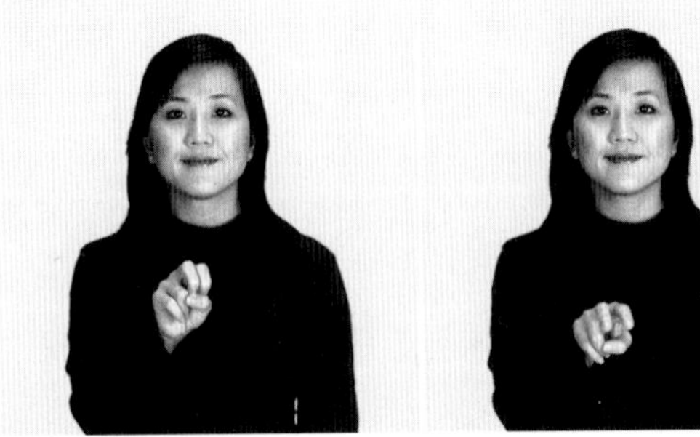

This sign is quite commonly used. It expresses the meaning of going on unchanged, as usual, still or like before. [refer to dialogue 2 in chapter 2]

Example: A and B are old friends. They have not seen each other for a long time, so they catch up on each other's news once they meet again. A asks B if she is still living in Mong Kok. B answers she still lives there. There has not been any change.

A : You/home/Mong Kok?/You?/~~?
B : Right!/I/~~.

Idiomatic sign 5

When a Deaf person has read another person's view and finds that view to be identical with his/her own or what he/she is going to express, this sign would be used to convey a meaning of convergence of view or total agreement.

Example: A and C are talking about the news that two Deaf friends have got married. C doesn't agree with A. So, A turns to B. After confirming that B shares the same view, A makes this sign.

A : <name sign>/<name sign>,/marry/finish?
B : right!/secretly/marry/finish!
A : ~~(one hand in front of B, the other hand in front of self)

第一課 Chapter 1

生活消閒 Leisure

收據	receipt
潮流/流行	trend/trendy
時髦/新潮	fashionable/stylish
性感	sexy
剪髮	hair cut
燙髮(曲髮)	perm hair (curly hair)
負離子直髮	ion hair-straightening
染髮	dye hair
塗指甲	fingernails
隱形眼鏡	contact lens
睇影碟	watching video disc
卡通	cartoon
遊戲機	video game (handy/home)
遊戲機(街機)	video game (at game centre)
的士高	disco
電單車	motor bike
豪華/富貴	luxury/wealthy
高級(餐廳、酒店等)	high class (e.g. restaurant, hotel)
通宵	overnight
宿營	camping in a resort/bungalow

對話 Dialogue

收據 receipt

潮流/流行 trend/trendy

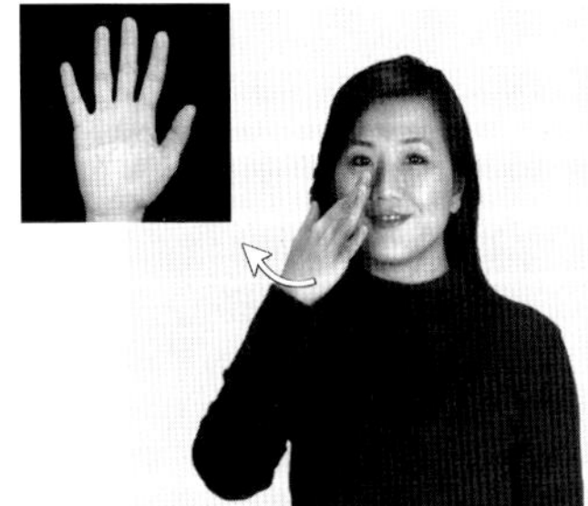

時髦/新潮 fashionable/stylish

性感 sexy

剪髮　hair cut

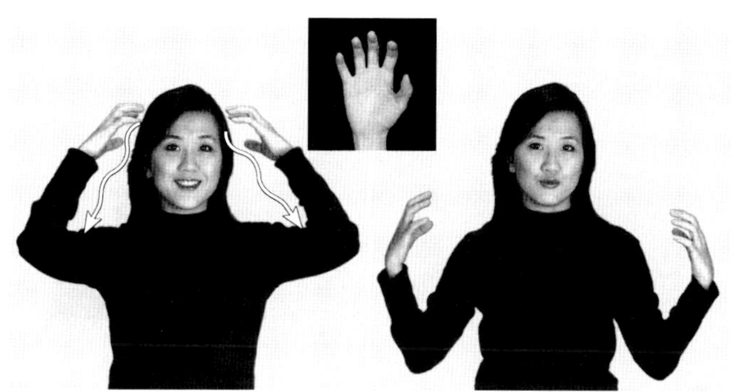

燙髮(曲髮)　perm hair (curly hair)

負離子直髮　ion hair-straightening

1

染髮　dye hair

塗指甲　fingernails

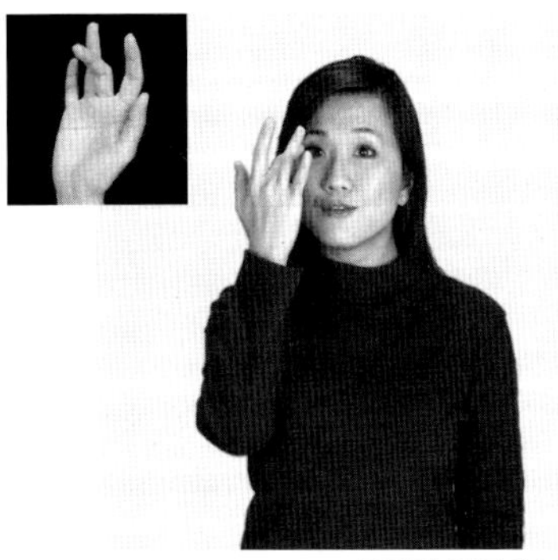

隱形眼鏡　contact lens

睇影碟 watching video disc

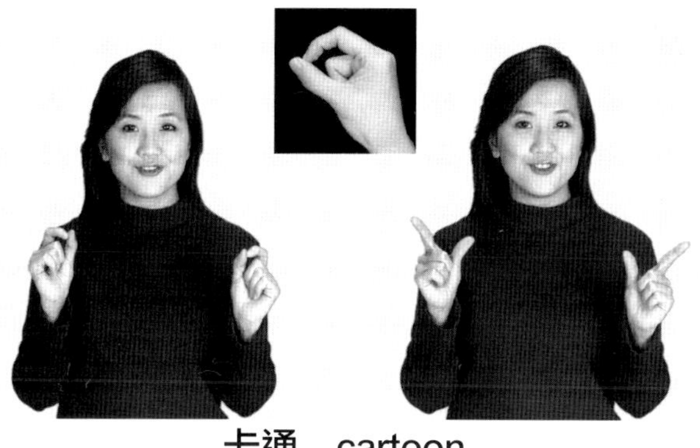

卡通 cartoon

遊戲機 video game (handy/home)

遊戲機(街機)
video game
(at game centre)

的士高　disco

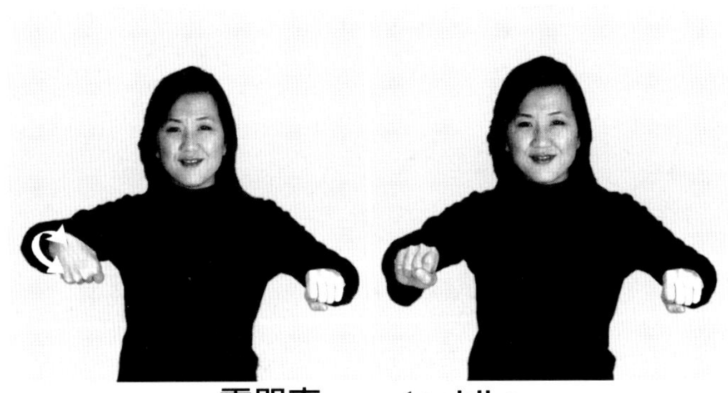

電單車　motor bike

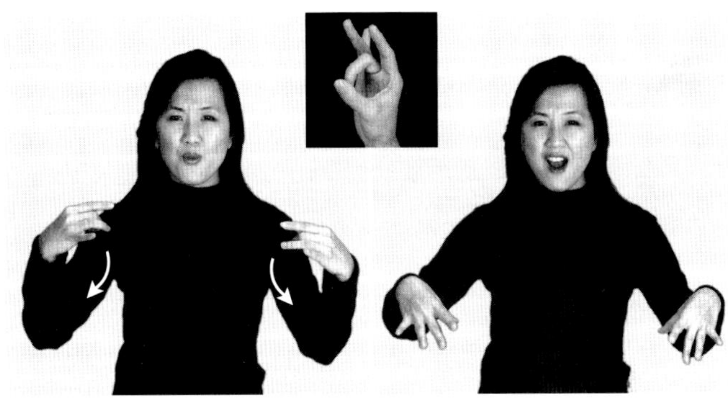

豪華/富貴　luxury/wealthy

高級(餐廳、酒店等)

high class (e.g. restaurant, hotel)

通宵　overnight

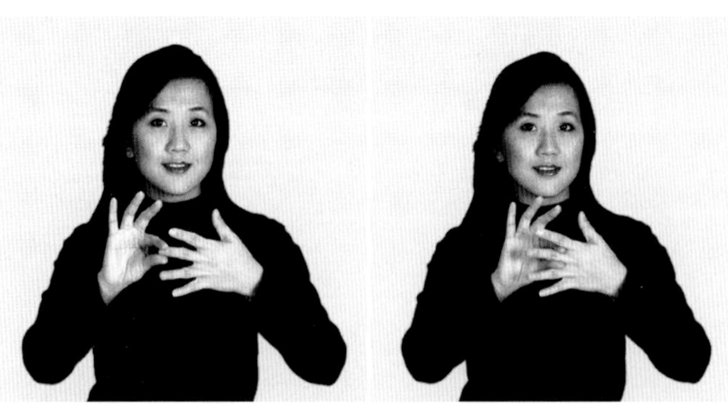

宿營　camping in a resort/bungalow

對話一

大減價

甲：　剛才我看報紙，見到崇光百貨公司的運動用品大減價呀！

乙：　不用了！只是九折這麼少。我有運動家的會員咭，有八折。

甲：　你沒有看過不知道，崇光百貨公司是半價呀！

乙：　半價？好，去看看。你想買什麼？

甲：　風褸，我最愛的Nike。你呢？

乙：　我看看再算，或者會買鞋，家裡很多鞋都已破舊了！

甲：　（突然想起）啊！我姨甥女生日，我打算買鞋送給她。

乙：　你知道她的尺碼？

甲：　知道！現在快去買吧！不然，恐怕很快賣完呢！

乙：　對！快去吧！

1 對話二

新髮型

甲： 你的新髮型（負離子直髮）不好看呢！還是以前曲髮比較好看。

乙： 你說得對！昨天我去髮型屋，見未試過負離子直髮，便試試看，怎料效果很差，很不適合我！

甲： 哦！你的新髮型花了多少錢？

乙： 很貴呀！要八百大元。

甲： 嘩！很貴呀！神經病！你太愚蠢了！

乙： 是的！我很愚蠢，很後悔，但都已成事實了，沒辦法！（突然發現）咦！你剪了留海？

甲： 是呀！昨天自己剪的。

乙： 真的想不到！你剪得很好看，你懂剪髮的嗎？

甲： 對呀！我懂的！去髮型屋剪髮太貴了，自己剪可以節省不少。

乙： 你說得對！你真厲害，會剪髮，我不會呢！

Dialogue 1

1

Big sales

A: I just read the newspaper and learnt that there is big sales of sports goods in Sogo Department Store.

B: No, thanks. But 10% off is so little. I have the membership card of Sportshouse and can enjoy 20% off.

A: You have not taken a look, that's why you don't know. It's half price offer at Sogo Department Store.

B: Half price? All right, let's go and take a look. What would you like to buy?

A: A windbreaker of my favourite brand Nike, and you?

B: I'll take a look first, perhaps I'll buy some shoes. Many shoes at my home are worn.

A: (Suddenly remember) Oh! It's my niece's birthday. I intended to buy a pair of shoes for her.

B: Do you know her size?

A: Yes, I do. Let's go and buy them quickly. Otherwise, I fear that they would be sold out quickly.

B: Right! Let's go quickly!

1 Dialogue 2

New hair-style

A: You don't look good with your new hair-style (ion hair-straightening). Your previous look with curly hair is prettier.

B: Your comment is right! Yesterday I went to a hair-salon. As I had never tried ion hair-straightening before, I gave it a try. Unexpectedly, it doesn't suit me at all!

A: I see! How much did you spend on your new hair-style?

B: It's very expensive! I paid 800 dollars!

A: Wow! It's so expensive! This is crazy! You are too stupid!

B: Yes, I was so stupid and I regret it. But it has already been done and there's nothing I can do!..... Oh! You have a fringe cut, haven't you?

A: Right! I cut it myself yesterday.

B: How surprising! You have cut it nicely. You know how to do a haircut, don't you?

A: Right! I do! It's too expensive to go to a hair salon. By cutting it myself, I can be thrifty.

B: You are right! You are so good with your hands by knowing how to do a haircut. I can't do it.

第二課　Chapter 2

運動 Sports

2

世界杯	World Cup
潛水	diving
划艇	rowing
壁球	squash
攀石	rock climbing
劍擊	fencing
滑板	skateboard
滑浪風帆	wind surfing
瑜珈	yoga
一比零	one to nil
打和	a draw
鬥	contend/compete against
勝利	win
頒獎	prize presentation
嘉賓	guest
觀眾	audience
開幕禮	opening ceremony
球証	referee
示範	demonstrate

對話 Dialogue

世界杯* World Cup*

潛水 diving

划艇 rowing

壁球* squash*

攀石 rock climbing

劍擊　fencing

1 2 3 4

滑板　skateboard

滑浪風帆　wind surfing

瑜珈　yoga

一比零　one to nil

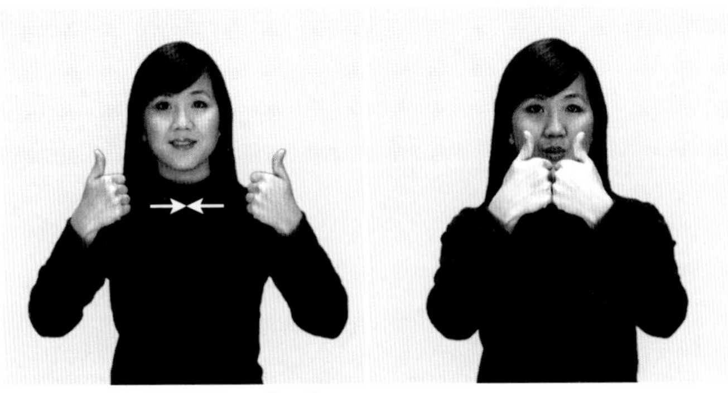

打和　a draw

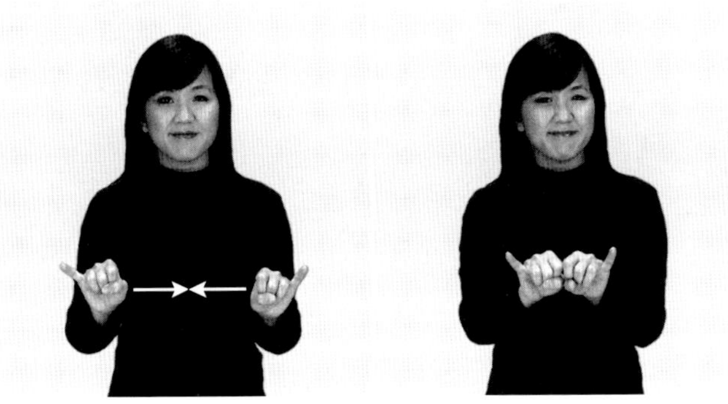

鬥　contend/compete against

勝利　win

2

頒獎* prize presentation*

嘉賓 guest

觀眾　audience

1　2

3　4

開幕禮*　opening ceremony*

球証 referee

示範 demonstrate

對話一

2

打壁球

甲： 我們倆人很久沒有見面了，大家都肥了！

乙： 對呀！因為我很久沒有運動了。

甲： 我也是。啊！不如我們去打壁球，你喜歡嗎？

乙： 我也是這樣想！以前我們一起去打壁球，很好玩呢！……但我家沒有球拍。

甲： 不用擔心！我的親戚有兩個球拍，可以問他借。

乙： 好！去哪裡打？要訂場嗎？

甲： 要呀！我家附近有場可以訂，如果有殘疾人士登記証，還可有優惠。

乙： 好呀！就這樣決定吧！你訂完場短訊給我吧！

甲： OK！

乙： OK！

對話二

2

行山

甲： 你是否瘦了？身體好像很弱。

乙： 是！我的身體很弱，但看你的身體很強壯呢！依舊有去行山嗎？

甲： 是啊！我經常去行山！很好玩的！你也來吧！

乙： 我不行的，我怕辛苦。

甲： 不用怕！你不用急，開始可以先行些容易的，等慢慢習慣後你便可以的了。

乙： 哦！明白了。你通常去哪裡行山的？

甲： 很多不同的地方，如西貢、大嶼山，有很多選擇呢！風景都很優美的。

乙： 好像不錯！我也想試試，你何時會去行山？

甲： 本星期日我們去行獅子山，很容易行，又舒服。來吧！

乙： 好！幾點？

甲： 早上九時半在黃大仙地鐵站恒生銀行等，OK？

乙： OK！本星期日見！

Dialogue 1

2

Let's play squash

A: We two have not seen each other for ages. We have both put on much weight!

B: Right! It's because I have not done any sports for a very long time.

A: Me too! Oh! Why don't we go and play squash, do you like it?

B: I am thinking about it too! In the past we played squash together. It was fun! But I don't have a racket at home.

A: Don't worry! My relative has two rackets. You can borrow one from him.

B: Good! Where shall we play squash? Do we need to book a court?

A: We do! There is a squash court available for booking near my home. If one can produce a Disability Registration Card, he will be eligible for a fee reduction.

B: Good! Done deal! Send me a SMS after you have booked the court.

A: OK!

B: OK!

Dialogue 2

2

Go hiking

A: Have you lost weight? You seem so weak.

B: Right! I am physically weak. But I can see that you are very strong. Do you still go hiking?

A: Yes! I often go hiking! It's fun! You too can come along!

B: I can't. I don't like the exertion.

A: Don't worry! You can take your time. At first you can walk some easy trails. When you get used to it in time, you will enjoy it.

B: Oh! I understand. Where do you usually go hiking?

A: Many different places, like Sai Kung and Lantau Island. There are many choices, the scenery of which is all good.

B: Sounds good! I would like to try, when will you go hiking?

A: This Sunday we are going hiking at Lion Rock. It's easy and comfortable. Come on!

B: Good! What time?

A: Let's meet up at 9:30a.m. at Wong Tai Sin MTR Hang Seng Bank, OK?

B: OK! See you this Sunday!

第三課 Chapter 3

飲食 Food and beverage

3

煮	cook
蒸	steam
炒	stir fry
炸	deep fry
煎	fry
餃子	dumpling
點心	dim sum
通粉	macaroni
腸粉	rice-roll
魷魚	squid
墨魚	cuttlefish
薑	ginger
沙律	salad
豆腐/啫喱	bean curd/jelly
芝士	cheese
漢堡飽	hamburger
薯條	french fries
普洱	puer tea
壽眉	shou mee tea
微波爐	microwave
焗爐	oven

選擇題練習 Multiple-choice Exercise

煮　cook

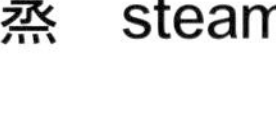

蒸　steam

炒　stir fry

3

炸* deep fry*

煎 fry

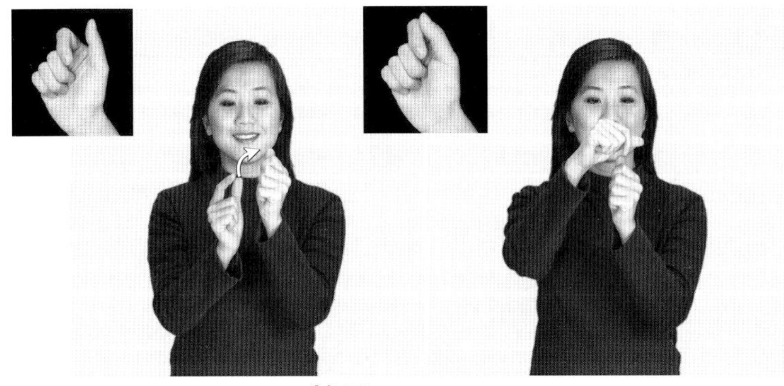

餃子 dumpling

點心 dim sum

通粉 macaroni

腸粉 rice-roll

魷魚 squid

墨魚 cuttlefish

薑　ginger

沙律*　salad*

豆腐/啫喱
bean curd/jelly

芝士　cheese

3

漢堡飽　hamburger

薯條　french fries

普洱　puer tea

壽眉　shou mee tea

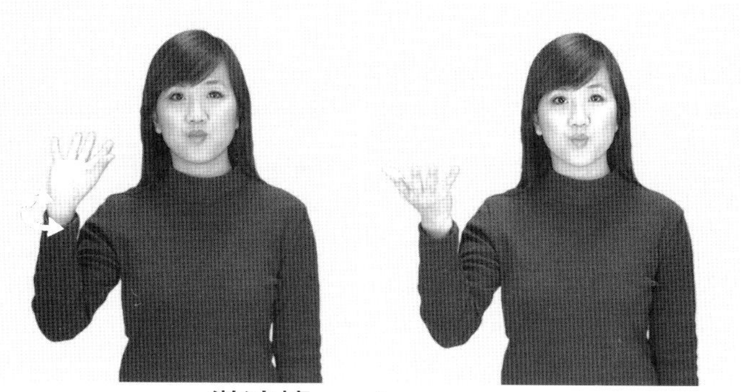

微波爐　microwave

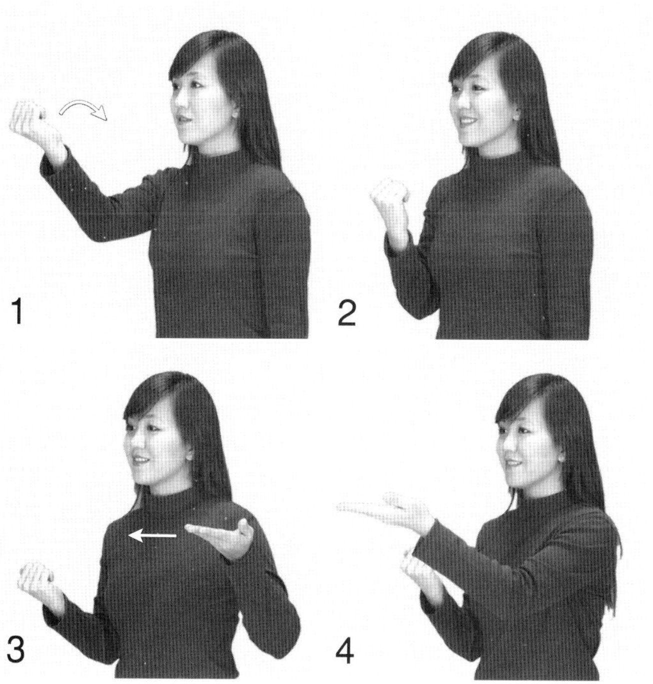

1

2

3

4

焗爐　oven

選擇題練習

請看影碟內的影片，然後圈出正確答案。

3

第1至4題，觀看影片中的描述，猜猜是什麼食物

選擇題1

1) A. 咕嚕肉　　B. 糖醋魚
   C. 中式牛柳　　D. 生炒骨

選擇題2

2) A. 青紅蘿蔔豬骨湯　　B. 蕃茄薯仔湯
   C. 蘿蔔薯仔牛骨湯　　D. 青紅蘿蔔瘦肉湯

選擇題3

3) A. 炸韮菜餃　　B. 蒸素菜餃
   C. 煎素菜餃　　D. 蒸菜肉餃

選擇題4

4) A. 什菜沙律　　B. 什果沙律
   C. 海鮮沙律　　D. 焗海鮮通粉

3

選擇題5-6

猜猜影片的主題是什麼？

5) A. 菜放多了醋怎麼辦　B. 菜放多了糖怎麼辦
   C. 菜放多了水怎麼辦　D. 菜放多了鹽怎麼辦

建議方法是：

6) A. 一大匙米醋和一大匙糖先拌勻，然後再倒入菜餚
   B. 先放一大匙米醋，然後放一大匙糖
   C. 先放一大匙糖，然後放一小匙米醋
   D. 一大匙米醋和一大匙水先拌勻，然後再倒入菜餚

選擇題7-8

影片中所描述的，是切什麼肉的方法？

7) A. 牛肉　B. 豬肉　C. 雞肉　D. 羊肉

建議把肉放在雪櫃的冰箱多久？

8) A. 15分鐘　B. 半小時　C. 1小時　D. 個半小時

Multiple-choice Exercise

Please watch the footage in the DVD and circle the correct option.

Questions 1 to 4, watch the footage and decide which food they depict.

MC Question 1

1) A. Sweet and sour pork
   B. Sweet and sour fish
   C. Chinese-style beef fillet
   D. Stir-fried spare ribs

MC Question 2

2) A. Soup of green carrot and red carrot plus pig bone
   B. Tomato and potato soup
   C. Soup of carrot and potato plus ox bone
   D. Soup and green turnip and carrot plus lean pork

MC Question 3

3) A. Deep-fried chives dumpling
   B. Steamed veggie-dumpling
   C. Fried veggie-dumpling
   D. Steamed cabbage and pork dumpling

MC Question 4

4) A. Assorted green salad
   B. Assorted green salad with fruit
   C. Seafood salad
   D. Baked seafood macaroni

3

MC Questions 5 & 6

What is the theme of the footage?

5) A. What we should do when we have put too much vinegar in the vegetables
   B. What we should do when we have put too much sugar in the vegetables
   C. What we should do when we have put too much water in the vegetables
   D. What we should do when we have put too much salt in the vegetables

The suggested solution is:

6) A. Prepare a well-mixed solution of one big spoon of rice-vinegar and one big spoon of sugar and then pour it onto the vegetables
   B. Put in a big spoon of rice-vinegar and then a big spoon of sugar
   C. Put in a big spoon of sugar and then a small spoon of rice-vinegar
   D. Prepare a well-mixed solution of one big spoon of rice-vinegar and a big spoon of water and then pour it onto the vegetables

MC Questions 7 & 8

According to the footage, what is the meat to be cut?

7) A. beef   B. pork   C. chicken   D. mutton

According to the footage, how long is the meat supposed to be left in the freezer compartment?

8) A. 15 minutes   B. half an hour
   C. one hour   D. one and a half hour

第四課 Chapter 4

資訊科技 Information technology

4

寬頻	broadband
視像對話	netmeeting
網頁	webpage
病毒	virus
檔案	file
列印	print
LCD顯示屏	LCD monitor
滑鼠	mouse
硬碟	hard disk
手提電腦	laptop
USB快閃儲存裝置	USB flash disk
燒錄光碟	burn disk
剪接	video editing
保養	maintenance
一倍	onefold
兩倍	twofold
火箭	rocket
太空人	astronaut
越來越多	increasing/becoming more and more
越來越少	decreasing/becoming less and less
發展	develop
人工耳蝸	cochlea implant

選擇題練習 Multiple-choice Exercise

寬頻　broadband

視像對話　netmeeting

網頁　webpage

病毒* virus*

4

檔案 file

列印 print

LCD顯示屏　LCD monitor

滑鼠　mouse

硬碟*　hard disk*

手提電腦* laptop*

USB快閃儲存裝置* USB flash disk*

燒錄光碟　burn disk

剪接　video editing

保養* maintenance*

一倍 onefold

兩倍 twofold

火箭　rocket

太空人*　astronaut*

4

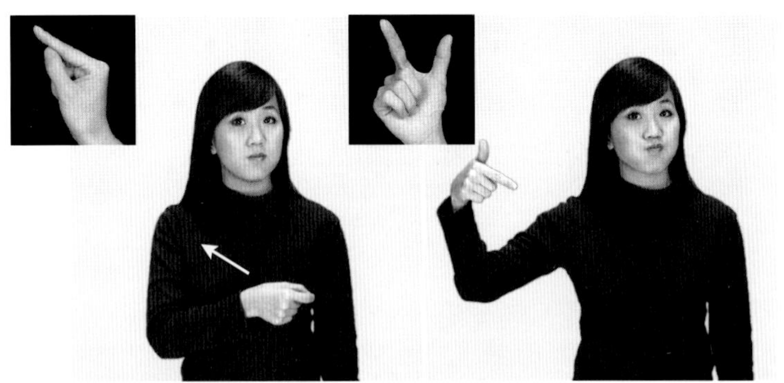

越來越多　increasing/becoming more and more

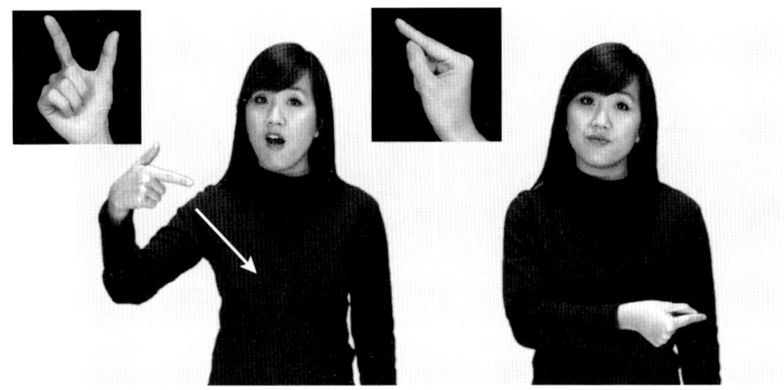

越來越少　decreasing/becoming less and less

發展　develop

人工耳蝸
cochlea implant

選擇題練習

請看影碟內的影片，然後圈出正確答案。

第1、2題，觀看影片中的描述，猜猜是哪一幅圖畫。

選擇題1

1) A.

B.

C.

D.

4

選擇題2

2) A.

B.

C.

D.

選擇題3-5

影片的主題是關於什麼？

3) A. 傳統助聽器與人工耳蝸　　B. 數碼助聽器

C. 傳統助聽器與數碼助聽器　　D. 數碼助聽器與人工耳蝸

數碼助聽器內部安裝了什麼？

4) A. 聲音放大器　　B. 微型電腦
C. 言語分析器　　D. 數碼噪音處理器

數碼助聽器的好處是：

5) A. 把所有聲音放大
B. 把環境噪音隔除，只保留言語聲
C. 把環境噪音降低，提升言語聲
D. 可以選擇不同聲音

4

選擇題6-8

影片提及的是哪兩個國家的科學家？

6) A. 英國及德國　　B. 法國及德國
C. 英國及法國　　D. 英國及俄國

科學家研究在哪裡安裝微型鏡頭？

7) A. 火車的座位上　　B. 火車的車箱內
C. 飛機的頭等客位上　　D. 飛機的座位上

安裝微型鏡頭可以監察什麼？

8) A. 乘客的睡姿　　B. 乘客的舉動和表情
C. 乘客的行為　　D. 乘客的交談內容

Multiple-choice Exercise

Please watch the footage in the DVD and circle the correct option.

Questions 1 & 2, watch the footage and decide which pictures they depict.

(Please refer to the pictures on page 47 and 48.)

4

MC Questions 3-5

What is the theme of the footage?

3) A. Conventional hearing aid and cochlea implant
   B. Digital hearing aid
   C. Conventional hearing aid and digital hearing aid
   D. Digital hearing aid and cochlea implant

What is installed in a digital hearing aid?

4) A. amplifier B. microcomputer
   C. language analyzer D. digital noise remover

The advantage of the digital hearing aid is that it:

5) A. amplifies all sounds
   B. filters voices from all background noises
   C. reduces background noises and enhances the output
   D. selects different sounds

MC Questions 6-8

The footage mentioned some scientists, which two countries are they from?

6) A. England and Germany B. France and Germany
   C. England and France D. England and Russia

4

The scientist are researching on the installation of pinhole cameras at which place?

7) A. train cabin seats
   B. train compartments
   C. first class compartments of airplanes
   D. airplane cabin seats

What would the pinhole cameras be monitoring?

8) A. the sleeping postures of the passengers
   B. the acts and expressions of passengers
   C. the behaviour of passengers
   D. the conversations of passengers

第五課　Chapter 5

旅遊 Travel

5

非洲	Africa
亞洲	Asia
首都	capital
直昇機	helicopter
坦克/捷克	tank/Czech
古老	ancient
護照	passport
簽証	travel visa
回鄉証	Home Entry Permit (booklet)
回鄉咭	Home Entry Permit (card)
入境事務處	Immigration Department
羅湖	Lo Wu
旅遊巴	coach [vehicle]
自助旅遊	self-organized tour
五星級	5-star
滑雪	skiing
降落傘	parachute
水上降落傘	parasailing
浸温泉	dipping in hot spring
笨豬跳	bungyjump

短文練習 Essay Practice

非洲 Africa

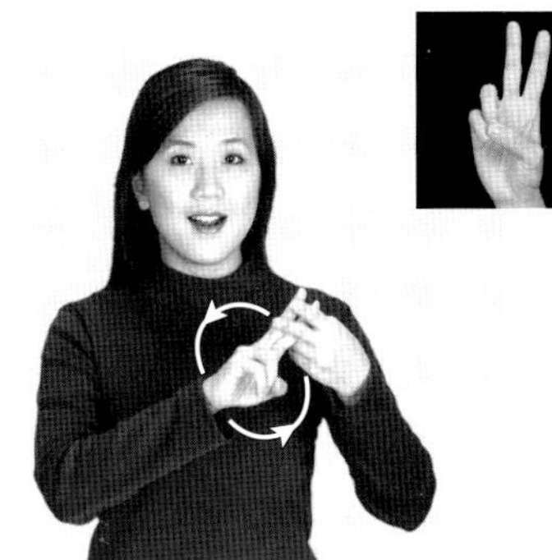

亞洲 Asia

首都 capital

直昇機 helicopter

坦克/捷克 tank/Czech

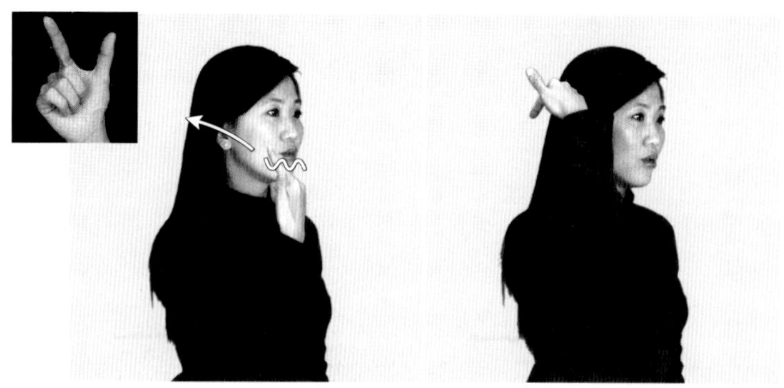

古老　ancient

5

護照　passport

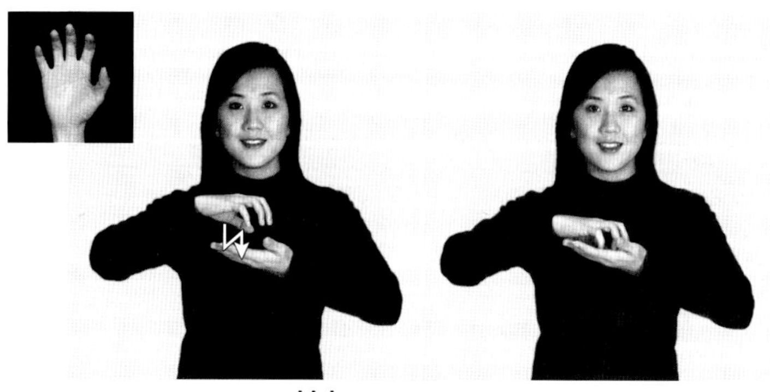

簽証　travel visa

回鄉証* Home Entry Permit (booklet)*

回鄉咭* Home Entry Permit (card)*

入境事務處* Immigration Department*

羅湖 Lo Wu

旅遊巴　coach [vehicle]

5

自助旅遊*　self-organized tour*

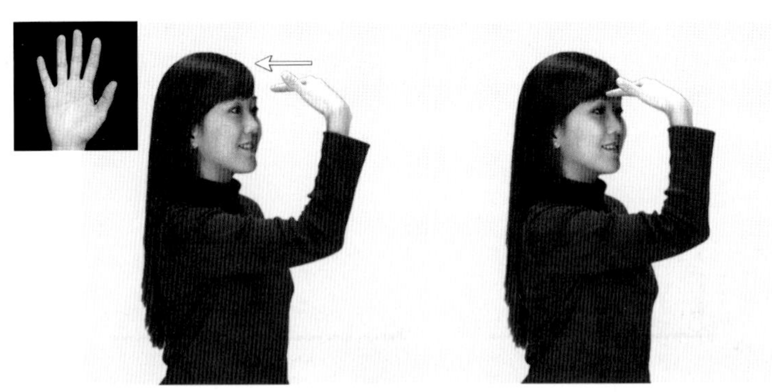

五星級　5-star

5

滑雪　skiing

降落傘　parachute

水上降落傘*　parasailing*

浸溫泉* dipping in hot spring*

笨豬跳 bungyjump

短文練習

短文練習1

上星期，世界最新的長途經濟航空公司在香港首航不順利。由於沒有飛越俄國上空的批准，該公司由香港飛往倫敦的航班在首天被逼取消。

資料來源：都市日報

5

短文練習2

旅客在辦理出境手續後，須接受保安檢查。為了節省檢查時間，保安檢查處備有透明塑料袋，讓旅客將隨身攜帶的金屬物品，如手提電話、鑰匙、硬幣、打火機，放進塑料袋內，以便進行X光檢查。

資料來源：香港國際機場網站

短文練習3

由一九九七年七月開始，凡享有香港特別行政區居留權及持有香港永久性居民身份證的中國公民，不論是否持有英國國民(海外)護照或香港身份證明書或其他旅行證件，俱可申請香港特別行政區護照。

資料來源：入境事務處網站

Essay Practice

Essay 1

The world's newest long-haul budget airline got off to an inauspicious start yesterday after its debut flight from Hong Kong to London was cancelled because it lacked permission to fly over Russia.

Info source: Metro News

Essay 2

At the security checking areas immediately after Immigration, passengers are given plastic bags to put all their metallic items, such as mobile phone, keys, coins and lighter, inside for x-ray screening to speed up the security process.

Info source: Hong Kong International Airport Website

Essay 3

Starting from July 1997, Chinese citizens with the right of abode (ROA) in the HKSAR and are holding Hong Kong permanent identity cards, whether or not they are holders of the "British National (Overseas) passport" or "Hong Kong Certificate of Identity" or other travel documents, are eligible to apply for the Hong Kong Special Administrative Region (HKSAR) passport.

Info source: Immigration Department Website

第六課　Chapter 6

社會文化 Society and Culture

6

移民	migrate
居留權	right of abode
圖書館	library
超級市場	supermarket
書法	calligraphy
陶瓷	ceramics
同性戀	homosexual
明星	movie star
習慣	accustomed to
六合彩	mark six
購物狂	shopaholics
投票	vote
抽籤	draw lots
手續費	handling fee
探訪	visit
交流	interact
環境	environment
分享	share
禮貌	courtesy

短文練習 Essay Practice

移民　migrate

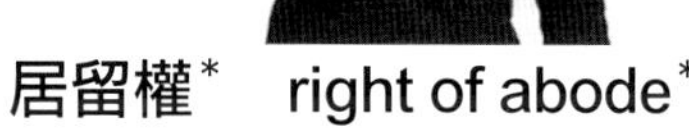

居留權*　right of abode*

圖書館　library

超級市場* supermarket*

6

書法 calligraphy

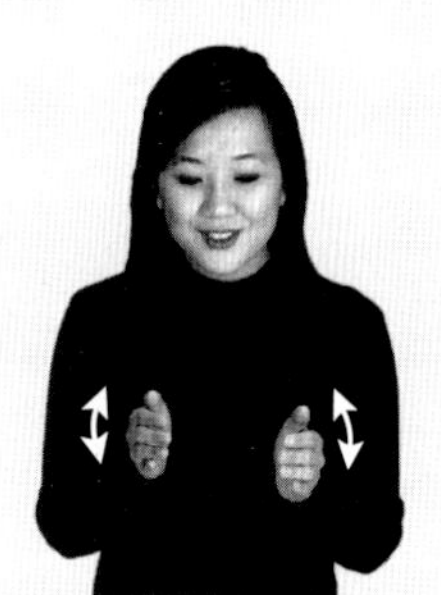

陶瓷 ceramics

同性戀 homosexual

明星　movie star

習慣　accustomed to

六合彩　mark six

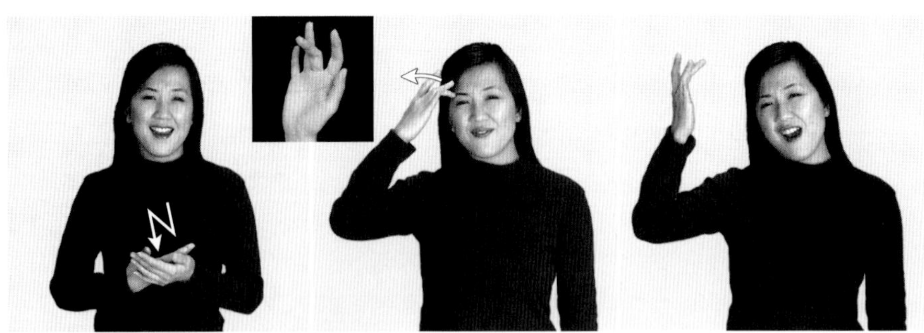

購物狂* shopaholics*

6

投票 vote

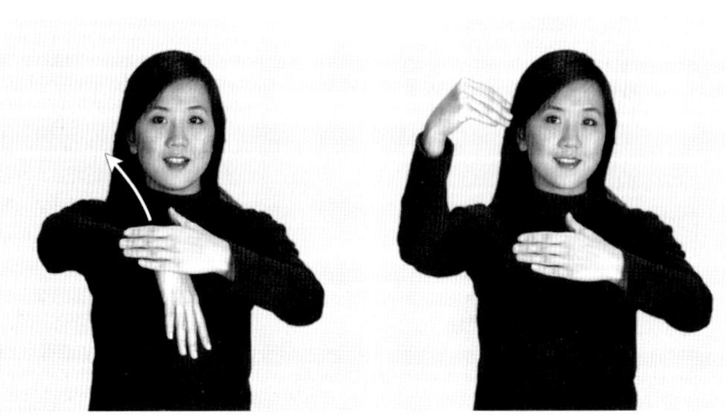

抽籤 draw lots

手續費* handling fee*

探訪 visit

交流 interact

環境 environment

分享　share

6

禮貌　courtesy

短文練習

短文練習1

人的一生有將近三分之一的時間花在睡眠上，剛出生的嬰兒幾乎每天都要睡二十個小時；即使成年後，每天至少要睡六至七小時，可見睡眠對我們是多麼重要。正因如此，我們不但要睡覺，還要睡得足夠、睡得有效率。

資料來源：生活晴報

短文練習2

農曆年將至，曲奇餅、朱古力、蛋卷等禮盒都是受歡迎的新春賀禮，有環保團體調查發現，近六成受訪者送賀禮時會用花紙包裝，但當收禮時，則有近九成人不介意禮盒沒有包裝。團體呼籲市民避免選購過度包裝的禮品，並再次建議政府參考外國例子，立法管制過度包裝。

資料來源：明報

短文練習3

香港人生活緊張，工作繁忙，加上科技進步，生活漸趨電子化，日常進行體力活動的機會越來越少，因此容易患上現代都市病，例如肥胖、糖尿病、高血壓、心臟病、失眠等。其實，運動對健康有莫大益處。你可選擇早一點起床，或利用吃午飯的時間，又或在晚飯前，從而改善健康狀況、提高工作效率，並配合世界的運動潮流。

資料來源：康樂及文化事務處網頁

Essay Practice

Essay 1

Man spends almost one third of his life on sleeping. A newborn infant spends almost 20 hours on sleeping every day. Even after we have grown up, we have to sleep at least six to seven hours each day. This shows how important sleeping is to us. Because of such importance, not only do we need to sleep, but we also need adequate and efficient sleep.

Info source: Mega Life Magazine

Essay 2

6

As Lunar New Year approaches, people will find boxes of cookies, chocolate or egg rolls to be popular festive gifts. A study conducted by an environmental protection organization reveals that nearly 60% of their interviewees would wrap their gifts when presenting them to others. However, when receiving gifts, about 90% of the interviewees say that they would not mind if the gifts are not wrapped. The organization calls upon the public not to buy gifts that are over-wrapped. Moreover, it again urges the government to follow the example of some foreign countries and pass laws against over-wrapping.

Info source: Ming Pao

Essay 3

Hong Kong people lead a tense life and are busily engaged in work. With technological advancement and computerization in our daily life, the chance of having physical activities regularly has been diminishing. Therefore, we are more susceptible to diseases such as obesity, diabetes, hypertension, heart disease and insomnia, which are commonly found in modern cities. In fact, physical activities are greatly beneficial to health. You may choose to get up earlier in the morning, or make use of lunchtime, or simply do exercise before dinner so as to improve your health and enhance efficiency. This habit will also tie in with the world's trend of taking regular exercise and enrich your life.

Info source: Leisure and Cultural Services Department website

第七課 Chapter 7

醫療健康 Medical and health

抽筋(全身)	spasm (general)
胃抽筋	gastric spasm
細菌	bacteria
痰	sputum
性交	sexual intercourse
避孕	contraception
結紮	ligation
量血壓	measure blood pressure
血壓	blood pressure
急救	first-aid
拯救	rescue
衰弱	weak
超聲波	ultrasound
X-光	X-ray
敏感	allergy
哮喘	asthma
傳染病	infectious disease
針灸	acupuncture
精神病	mental illness
輪椅	wheelchair
蚊	mosquito
蟑螂	cockroach

觀看理解練習 Comprehension Exercise

抽筋(全身)　spasm (general)

胃抽筋*　gastric spasm*

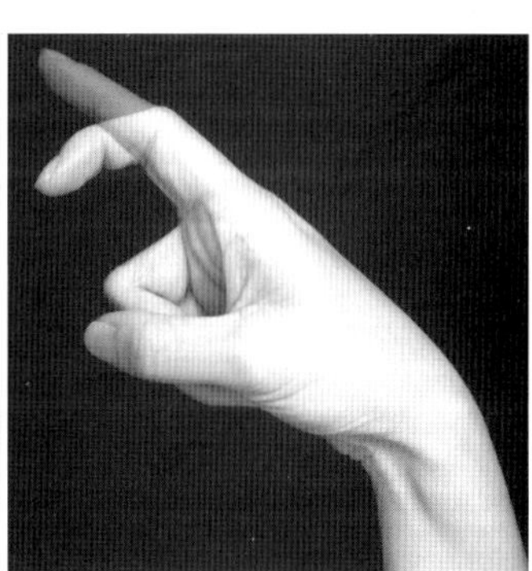

細菌　bacteria

痰* sputum*

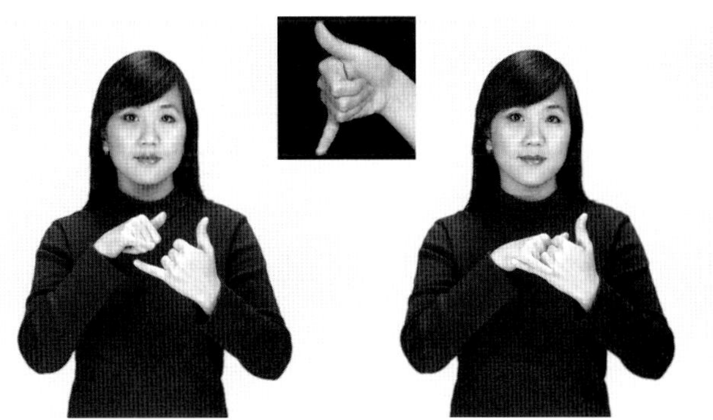

性交 sexual intercourse

避孕* contraception*

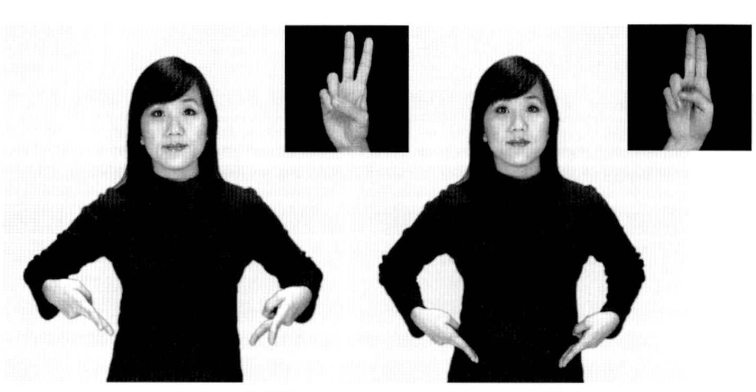

結紮 ligation

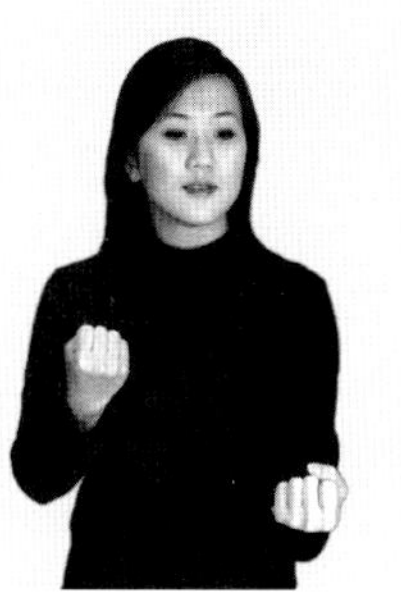

量血壓　measure blood pressure

血壓*　blood pressure*

7

急救　first-aid

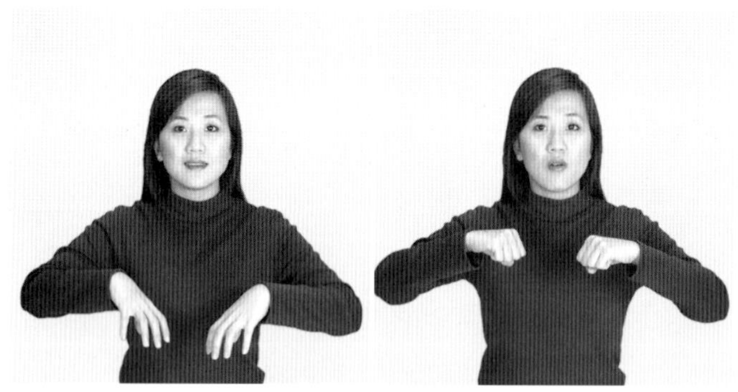

拯救　rescue

衰弱　weak

超聲波　ultrasound

7

X-光*　X-ray*

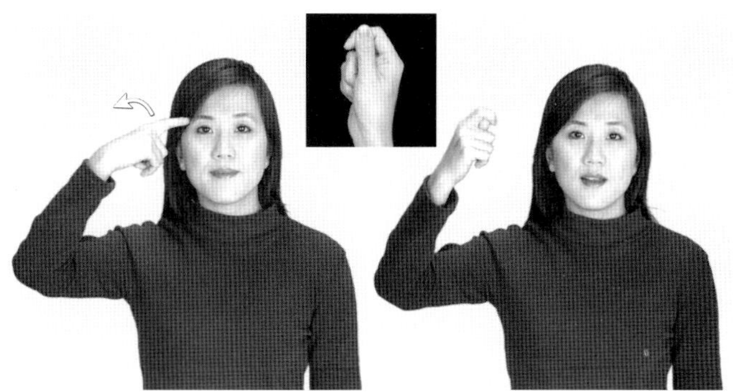

敏感　allergy

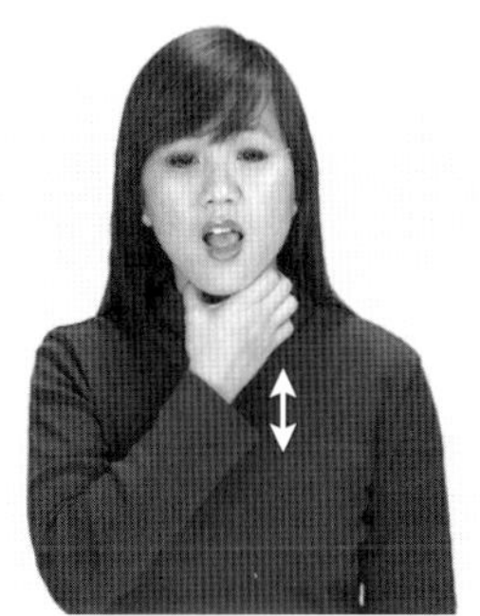

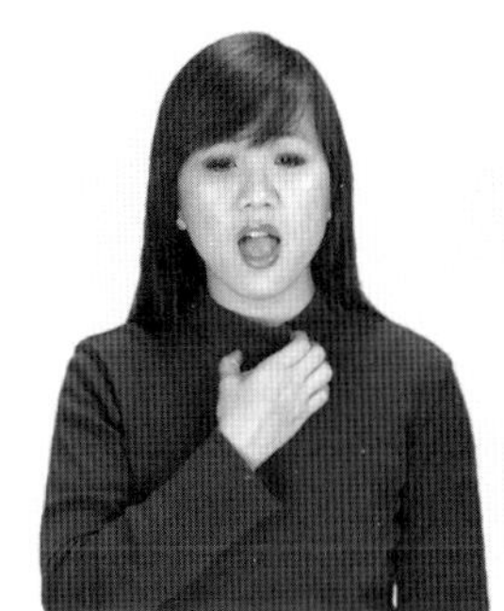

哮喘　asthma

7

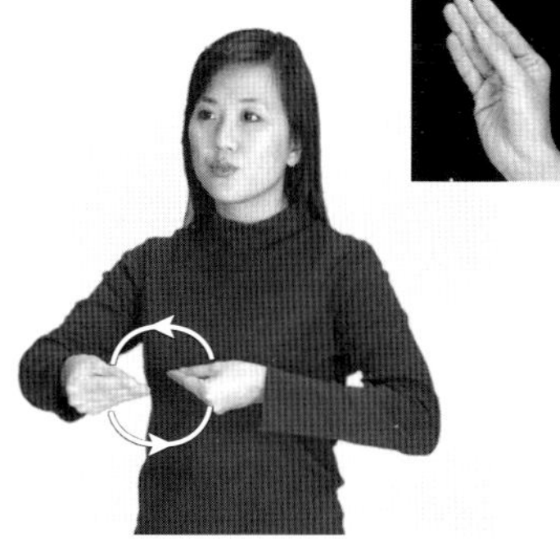

傳染病*　infectious disease*

針灸　acupuncture

精神病*　mental illness*

7

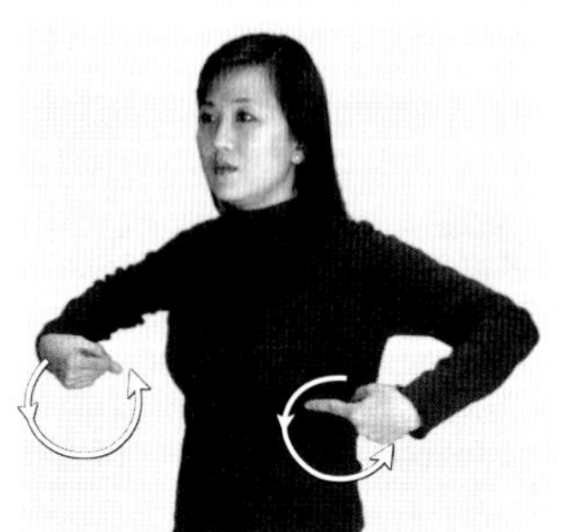

輪椅　wheelchair

蚊* mosquito*

蟑螂 cockroach

觀看理解練習

留心觀看影碟內的片段，然後回答以下問題：

1) 研究發現，每天進行多少分鐘中等劇烈程度的運動，可以促進健康？

2) 為什麼很多人都沒有做運動的習慣？

3) 影片建議怎樣將運動融入我們日常生活當中？

4) 行樓梯可以在什麼地點和時間進行？

5) 每天行樓梯可減低患上冠心病、高血壓、結腸癌和什麼病的機會呢？

6) 如患有心臟病或呼吸系統等慢性疾病，開始運動計劃要留意什麼？

Comprehension Exercise

Watch the footage in the disc and answer the following questions:

1) According to studies, how many minutes of physical activity of moderate intensity every day is beneficial to health?

2) Many people do not exercise regularly, why?

3) In order to incorporate physical activity into daily life, what does the footage suggest?

4) Where and when can stair-climbing be done?

5) Daily stair-climbing reduces the risk of developing coronary heart disease, hypertension, colon cancer and what?

6) If one is suffering from a chronic disease like heart disease or respiratory disease, what should one do before starting the exercise program?

第八課 Chapter 8

就業．經濟 Employment and economics

賠償〔名詞〕/追討(賠償、欠款等)	compensation/to urge someone to make compensation/payment
損失/吃虧	suffer losses/at a disadvantage
破產/失業	bankrupt/unemployed
曠工/曠課	skip work/school
兼職	part-time job
散工	odd jobs
湊錢/合資	to pool money/club together
公費	public funds
機會	opportunity
獎金	bounty
阻礙	an obstacle/ to hinder
評核/評判	assess/judge
懲罰	punish
成立(公司、機構等)	set up (a company, an organisation, etc)
成立(小組、委員會等)	to form (a group,a committee, etc)
委託	entrust
股票	stocks
消息	tidings
複雜	complex
解釋	explain
發生	happen

觀看理解練習 Comprehension Exercise

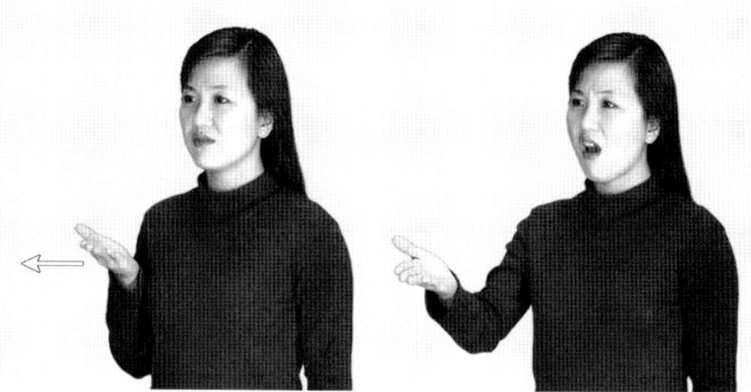

賠償[名詞]/追討(賠償、欠款等)
compensation/to urge someone to make compensation or payment

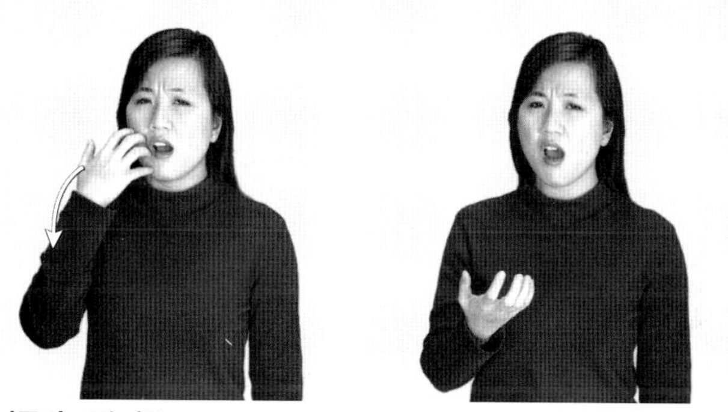

損失/吃虧 suffer losses/at a disadvantage

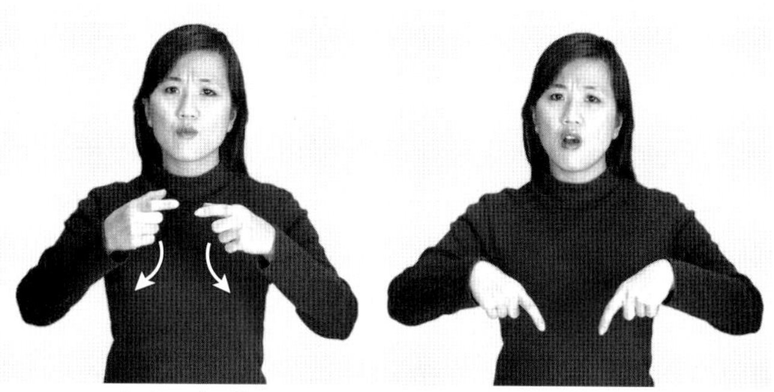

破產/失業 bankrupt/unemployed

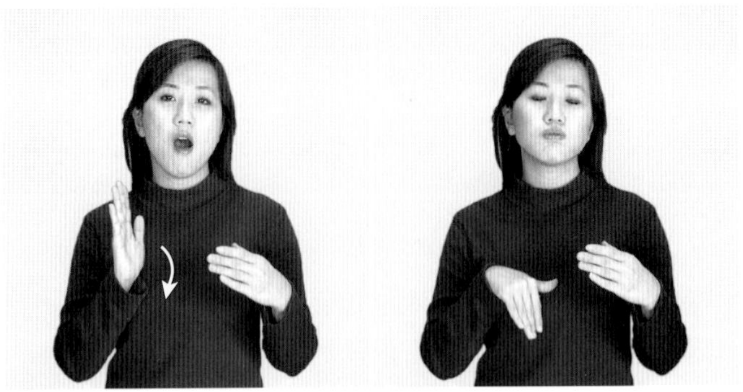
曠工/曠課　skip work/skip school

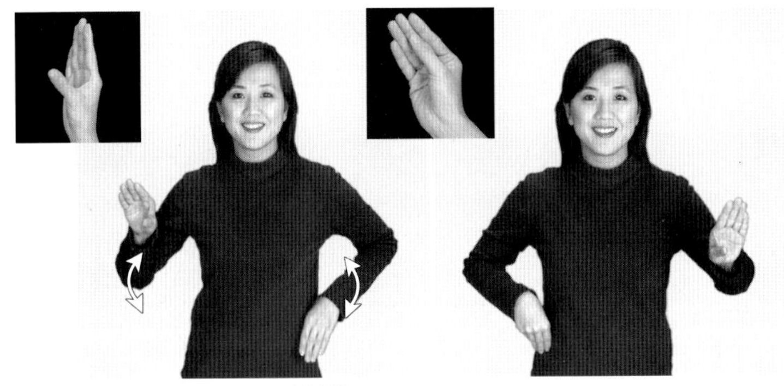
兼職　part-time job

8

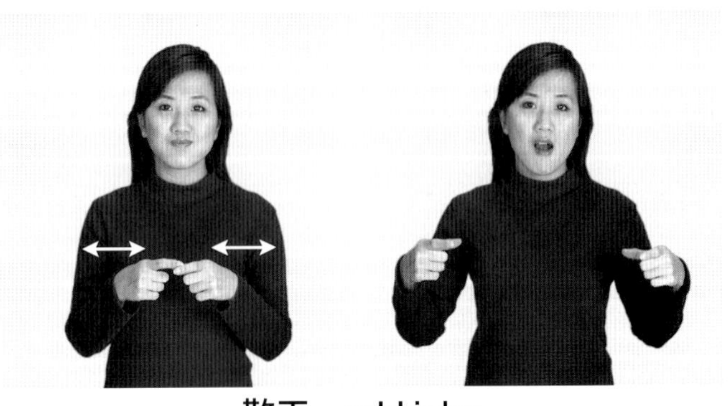
散工　odd jobs

湊錢/合資　to pool money/club together

公費　public funds

8

機會　opportunity

8

獎金* bounty*

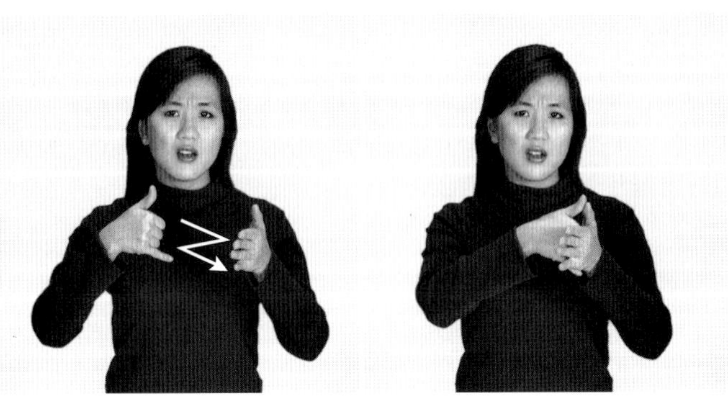

阻礙 an obstacle/ to hinder

評核/評判 assess/judge

懲罰 punish

成立(公司、機構等)
set up (a company, an organisation, etc)

8

成立(小組、委員會等)
to form (a group,a committee, etc)

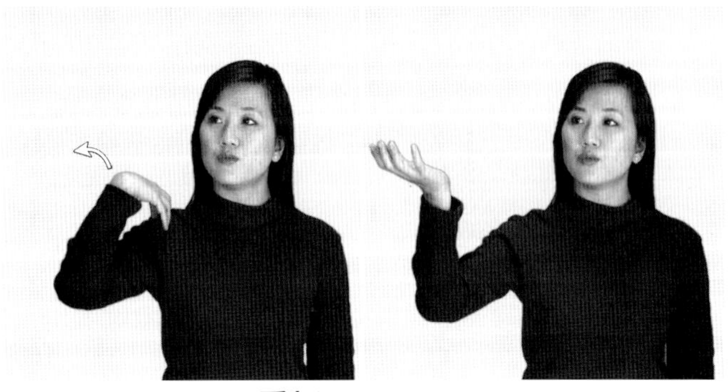

委託　entrust

股票* stocks*

消息 tidings

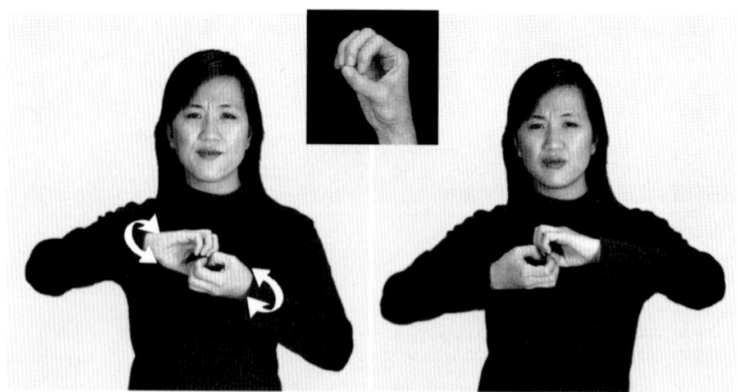

複雜　complex

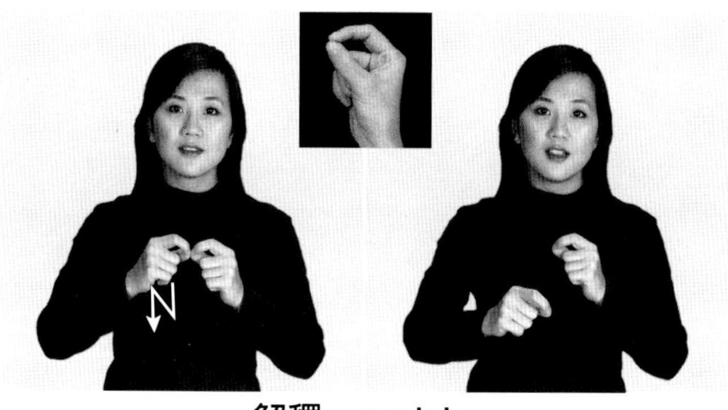

解釋　explain

8

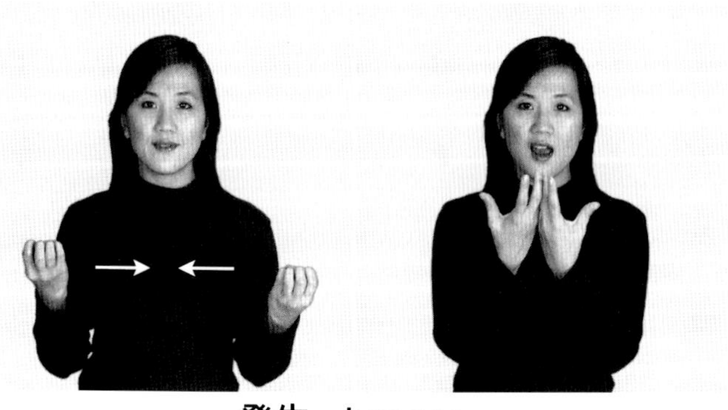

發生　happen

觀看理解練習

留心觀看影碟內的片段，然後回答以下問題：

1) 勞工處展能就業科自何年何月起推出「就業展才能計劃」？

2) 僱主為殘疾求職者提供的試工期為多少個月？

3) 「就業展才能計劃」除了給予殘疾求職者試工機會外，還有什麼服務？

4) 在試工期間，負責委派指導員的是展能就業科？還是僱主？

5) 每聘用一位求職者，僱主每月可獲得的工資補助金額最高是？

6) 為表謝意，指導員為殘疾員工提供在職輔導，可獲贈獎勵金多少元？

7) 九龍區的查詢傳真號碼是：

8) 新界區的查詢電話號碼是：

Comprehension Exercise

Watch the footage in the disc and answer the following questions:

1) When did the Selective Placement Division of the Labour Department launch the Work Orientation and Placement Scheme (WOPS)?

2) How long is the work trial period offered by the employer to the disabled job-seeker?

3) Apart from giving a chance for disabled job-seekers to do a work trial, what other service is the Work Orientation and Placement Scheme offering?

4) During the work trial period, which party will be responsible for appointing a mentor? The Selective Placement Division or the employer?

5) What is the maximum monthly amount of financial incentive receivable by an employer for engaging a job-seeker?

6) As a token of appreciation, how much cash award will be given to a mentor for assisting a disabled employee?

7) The enquiry fax number for Kowloon office is:

8) The enquiry phone number for New Territories Office is:

第九課 Chapter 9

情緒，行為，感受 Emotion, behaviour and feeling

跟隨	follow
依賴	rely on
欺負	bully
支持	support
照顧	look after
監視	watch closely
強迫	compel
利用	make use of
反叛	rebellious
不聽話	disobedient
不理睬	ignore
不耐煩	impatient
歧視	discriminate
偏心	biased
固執	stubborn
後悔	repent
放棄	give up
鼓勵	encourage
主動	active
暗戀	loving someone secretly
性格	personality

跟隨 follow

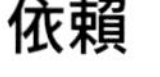

依賴 rely on

欺負 bully

支持　support

照顧　look after

9

監視　watch closely

強迫　compel

利用　make use of

反叛　rebellious

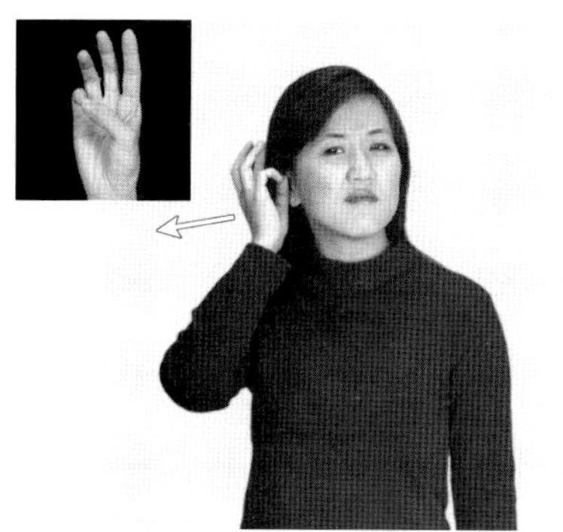

不聽話　disobedient

不理睬　ignore

9

不耐煩　impatient

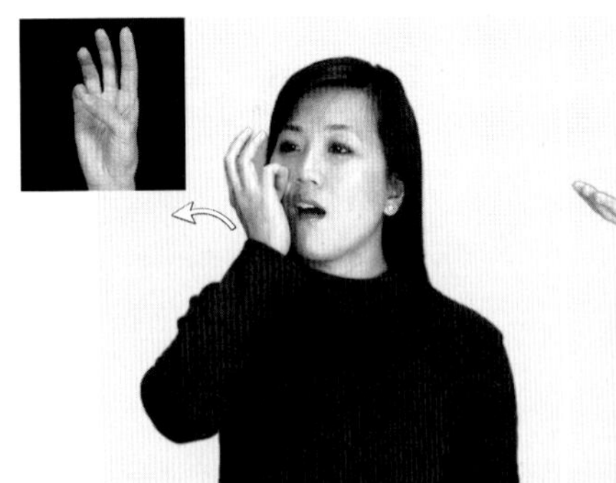

歧視　discriminate

偏心　biased

9

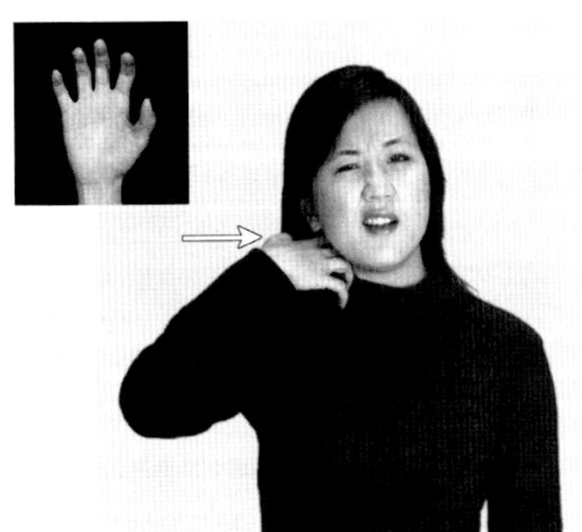

固執　stubborn

後悔　repent

放棄　give up

鼓勵　encourage

9

主動　active

暗戀　loving someone secretly

性格　personality

第十課 Chapter 10

時事新聞 Current affairs

新聞	news
電視新聞	TV news
無線電視	TVB
亞洲電視	ATV
有線電視	Cable TV
香港電台	RTHK
訪問/記者	interview/reporter
意外	accident
示威	demonstration
士兵	soldier
軍隊	army
偷渡入境	illegal immigration
偷渡出境/逃走	illegal emigration/escape
地震	earthquake
水浸	flood
毒品/吸毒	dangerous drug/taking dangerous drug
謀殺	murder
貪污	corruption
非禮/好色	indecent assault/lusty
充公	confiscation
調查	investigate

新聞* news*

電視新聞 TV news

無線電視　TVB

亞洲電視　ATV

有線電視*　Cable TV*

香港電台* RTHK*

訪問/記者 interview/reporter

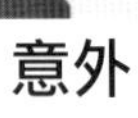
意外 accident

示威 demonstration

士兵 soldier

軍隊* army*

偷渡入境 illegal immigration

偷渡出境/逃走　illegal emigration/escape

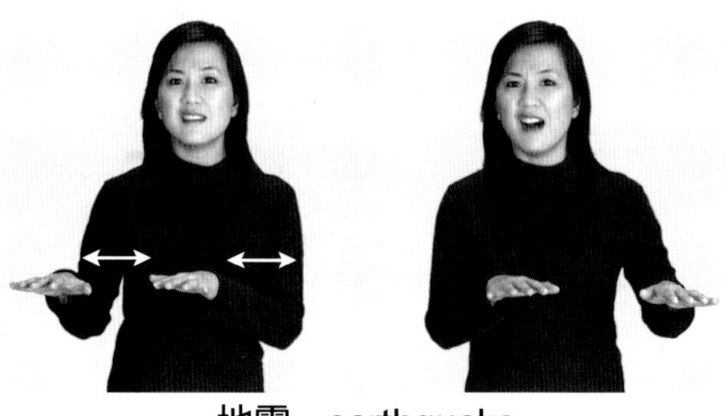
地震　earthquake

10

水浸　flood

毒品/吸毒

dangerous drug/taking dangerous drug

謀殺 murder

貪污* corruption*

非禮/好色　indecent assault/lusty

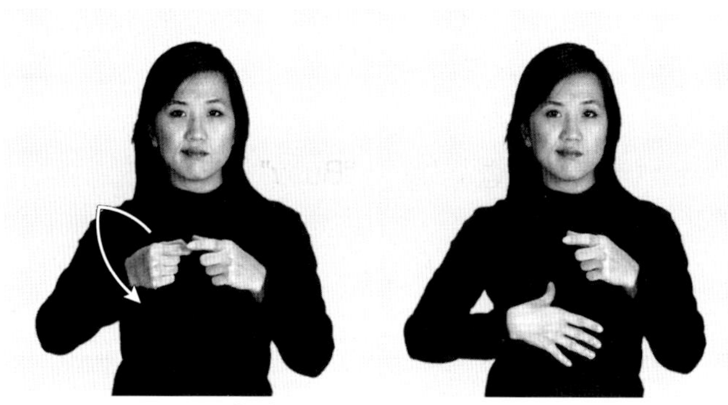

充公　confiscation

10

調查　investigate

練習答案 Answers

第三課 Chapter 3

1) A	2) D	3) B	4) C
5) D	6) A	7) A	8) B

第四課 Chapter 4

1) B	2) D	3) C	4) B
5) C	6) A	7) D	8) B

第七課 Chapter 7

三十分鐘	(1)	30 minutes
很忙	(2)	"Busy"
行樓梯	(3)	stair climbing
幾乎任何地點和時間都可以	(4)	almost anywhere and anytime
糖尿病	(5)	diabetes
應先請教醫生	(6)	consult a doctor first

第八課 Chapter 8

2005年4月	(1)	April 2005
3個月	(2)	3 months
職前培訓	(3)	pre-employment training programme
僱主	(4)	the employer
$3000	(5)	$3000
$500	(6)	$500
2796 0369	(7)	2796 0369
2417 6190	(8)	2417 6190

影片原稿

第三課

選擇題5-6

菜放太多鹽怎麼辦

炒菜的時候，不小心鹽放多了，或醬油過量而導致菜太鹹怎麼辦？千萬別加水煮成湯或把汁液沖掉，正確的方法是：用一大匙米醋、一大匙糖先拌勻，再倒入菜餚內炒勻，這樣就可以去除太鹹的困擾了。

資料來源：今日美食網

選擇題7-8

切牛肉先冷凍

切牛肉絲或牛肉片時，可將整塊的牛肉包好，平整的放入雪櫃冷凍庫冰凍半小時，待外形凍硬固定時，再取出切割，便容易多了。因為未經冰凍的牛肉，質地軟而易黏刀，無法切割順手，冰過便比較好切。

資料來源：今日美食網

第四課

選擇題3-5

傳統助聽器與數碼助聽器

傳統助聽器本質上就是小型聲音放大器，對聲音放大沒有選擇，對人們需要的言語聲，音樂聲等放大，同時也對不需要的噪音進行放大，因此在嘈雜環境中，聽取效果受到較大的影响。數碼助聽器是在內部安裝了一台微型電腦，能根據佩戴者的聽力損失特點和要求，自動地對聲音進行處理，能有效地降低噪音，提升言語聲，大大提高了言語的清晰度和保真性。

資料來源：中國助聽訊息網

選擇題6-8

英研飛機座位裝微型鏡頭反恐

英國及德國的科學家研究在飛機的座位上安裝微型鏡頭，監察每個乘客的一舉一動及面部表情，以分析其是否恐怖份子，務求及早阻止劫機或引爆炸彈等襲擊。

資料來源：明報

第七課

運動與健康-行樓梯

研究發現，每天進行三十分鐘中等劇烈程度的運動，可以促進健康。它有助控制體重，更有益心理、生理及社交方面的健康。然而，很多人都沒有做運動的習慣，因為他們「很忙」。其實您應該盡量找機會多做運動。行樓梯就是將運動融入日常生活的方法之一。行樓梯是既方便又容易做到的運動，適合大部份人士。對缺乏運動的人士來說，尤其容易達到。

建議

- 如情況合適，盡量行樓梯，以代替乘搭升降機或電梯。
- 上班或回家時，行幾層樓梯。

行樓梯的好處

慢慢行樓梯，對大部份人來說都是極佳的運動。行樓梯幾乎任何地點和時間都可以進行，而且所費無幾，容易做到。每天行樓梯，對健康有莫大裨益：

- 使體格強健，有效強化心臟及血管。
- 改善心肺功能及血液循環。
- 減低患上冠心病、高血壓、糖尿病及結腸癌的機會。
- 增強身體抵抗力，減低患病機會，從而提升工作效率。
- 使骨骼強健，減低患上骨質疏鬆症的機會。
- 強化肌肉。
- 燃燒脂肪，有助控制體重。

但是，如有以下情況，開始運動計劃前應先請教醫生：

- 患有慢性疾病，例如心臟病、呼吸系統疾病。
- 運動時或運動後感到胸部疼痛或不適。
- 容易因頭暈而失去知覺。
- 稍費力氣已覺呼吸困難。
- 已屆中年或以上，一直沒有運動，現計劃從事較為劇烈的運動。
- 有骨骼或關節毛病，例如關節出現紅腫、發熱、疼痛或僵硬等徵狀。

資料來源：衛生署網頁

第八課

「就業展才能計劃」

勞工處展能就業科自二零零五年四月推出「就業展才能計劃」，透過職前培訓和試工機會，以提升殘疾人士的就業競爭力，並鼓勵僱主親身體驗及了解他們的工作能力。

計劃簡介

為殘疾求職者提供職前培訓，協助他們掌握最新的勞工市場資訊、求職策略、面試技巧、工作操守，以及人際關係／溝通技巧等。
僱主為殘疾求職者提供為期三個月的試工。試工期滿後，僱主可自行決定是否繼續聘用有關員工。
在試工期間，展能就業科鼓勵僱主委派一名資深的員工擔任指導員，協助試工僱員掌握工作技巧及適應工作環境，並與同事融洽相處。

工資補助/獎勵項目

每聘用一位求職者，僱主可獲得工資補助，金額相等於殘疾僱員的工資的一半（最高以每月港幣三千元為限），最長為期三個月。
除了獲得工資補助外，僱主如在僱員完成三個月的試工後繼續聘用該僱員，將獲頒發銘謝狀，以表彰其聘用殘疾僱員的開明態度。
指導員為殘疾員工提供在職輔導，可獲贈獎勵金伍佰元，以表謝意。
完成三個月試工的殘疾僱員，會獲頒發嘉許狀，以茲鼓勵。

參加辦法及查詢

如果你想透過「就業展才能計劃」聘用殘疾人士，可下載有關表格，填妥後並傳真至本科的展能就業科分區辦事處。我們的就業主任會儘快為你提供專業的就業選配及引薦服務。如有進一步查詢，歡迎與我們聯絡。

香港區
電話：2852 4801
傳真：2541 5290

九龍區
電話：2755 4835
傳真：2796 0369

新界區
電話：2417 6190
傳真：2499 3713

資料來源：勞工處網頁

Footage Scripts

Chapter 3

MC Questions 5 & 6

What we should do when there is too much salt in the stir-fried vegetable.

What should we do if we have put too much salt or sauce when stir-frying some vegetables? Do not add in water to make soup or simply drain the juice. The correct way of handling the situation is to prepare a well-mixed solution of one big spoon of rice-vinegar and one big spoon of sugar and then pour it onto the vegetables in the wok. Stir well. This would remove the risk of the dish getting too salty.

Info source: FoodNo1.com

MC Questions 7 & 8

Freeze the beef before cutting it

Before shredding or cutting beef into fillets, you can wrap the slab of beef and put it horizontally into the freezer compartment of the fridge for half an hour. When the outer surface of the slab becomes hardened, take it out for cutting. The cutting would become much easier. When left in room temperature, the beef would be soft and may get stuck on the blade, thus hindering the movement of the knife. The cutting would be smoother when the beef has been left in low temperature for some time.

Info source: FoodNo1.com

Chapter 4

MC Questions 3-5

Conventional hearing aid and digital hearing aid

The conventional hearing aid is basically a miniature amplifier, sounds are amplified indiscriminately; no matter they are voices, lovely music or nuisance noises. Consequently, in a noisy environment, the quality of its output is often affected. On the other hand, the digital hearing aid has in itself a microcomputer, which enables the device to instantly adjust the output according to the hearing impairment and input-preference of the user. As a result, the clarity and authenticity of the voices and sound output are enhanced by effectively reducing the background noises.

Info source: China hearing aid net

MC Questions 6-8

British researches on installation of cabin pinhole cameras as a counter-terrorism measure

British and German scientists are researching on the installation of pinhole cameras at airplane cabin seats so as to monitor the acts and facial expressions of individual passengers in order to analyze the possible presence of terrorists. It is hoped that such measures can effectively neutralize attacks such as hi-jacking or bomb detonation.

Info source: Ming Pao

Chapter 7

Exercise and Health - Stair Climbing

Studies reveal that 30 minutes of physical activity of moderate intensity everyday is beneficial to health. It helps you to control body weight and is good for your psychological, physical and social health. Many people do not exercise regularly because they are "busy". However, you should try your best to find opportunity to exercise more. Stair climbing is one of the ways of incorporating physical activity into daily life. It is a convenient and easily accessible exercise for the majority of people, especially the sedentary people.

Suggestion

- Use stairs instead of elevators or escalators if possible.
- Walk a few flights of stairs when you go to work or go home.

Benefits of Stair Climbing

Taken slowly, climbing stairs can be an excellent form of workout for the majority of people. You can do it almost anywhere and anytime. It is a low-cost and readily accessible form of exercise that provides a series of health benefits if we do it everyday.

- It builds up body strength and cardiovascular endurance.

- It enhances heart and lung function and improves blood circulation.
- It reduces the risk of developing coronary heart disease, hypertension, diabetes or colon cancer.
- It increases body resistance, thus reduces the chance of contracting diseases and increases efficiency at work.
- It leads to healthy bones and lowers the risk of osteoporosis.
- It strengthens muscles.
- It decreases body fat, thereby controlling body weight.

However, before starting the exercise program, you should consult a doctor if:

- you have chronic medical disease, e.g. heart disease, respiratory disease.
- you experience chest pain or discomfort during or right after exercise.
- you tend to lose consciousness due to dizziness.
- you feel shortness of breath after mild exertion.
- you are middle-aged or older, have not been physically active and plan a relatively vigorous exercise program.
- you have joint problems, e.g. you experience pain, aching, stiffness or swelling in or around a joint.

Info source: Department of Health Website

Chapter 8

Work Orientation and Placement Scheme

With a view to enhance the employability and competitiveness of people with disabilities through pre-employment training and work placement, the Selective Placement Division of the Labour Department has launched the Work Orientation and Placement Scheme (WOPS) in April 2005. The Scheme also aims to encourage employers to better understand the working abilities of people with disabilities.

The Scheme

Under the Scheme, a pre-employment training programme will be offered to each participating disabled job-seeker, covering the latest job market information, job-search skills, interviewing techniques, work ethics, communication/interpersonal skills, etc.

The participating employer will offer a three-month work trial to the

disabled job-seeker and will be free to decide whether to continue the employment upon completion of the work trial period.
The participating employer is encouraged to appoint an experienced staff as the Mentor of the disabled employee. During the work trial period, the Mentor will coach the disabled employee on relevant job skills, as well as assist him to adapt to the new job and integrate with co-workers.

Incentive/Awards

A Financial Incentive will be paid to the participating employer for up to 3 months in respect of each disabled person engaged (amount being equal to 50% of the actual wages paid to the disabled employee, subject to a ceiling of $3000 per month)
A Certificate of Appreciation, in addition to the financial incentive, will be awarded to every employer who continues to employ the disabled employee after the three-month work trial period as a recognition of the former's enlightened employment policy.
A Cash Award of $500, as a token of appreciation, will be given to every Mentor who has assisted the disabled employee to continue with the work trial after the first month.
A Certificate of Commendation, as a token of encouragement, will be presented to every disabled employee who has successfully completed the three-month work trial.

Application & Enquiry

If you wish to recruit disabled job-seekers through WOPS, please download the application form and return the completed application form by facsimile to the respective regional office of the Selective Placement Division. Our placement officers will provide you with professional job matching/referral services promptly. For further enquiry, please contact our colleagues at:

Hong Kong Office	**Kowloon Office**	**New Territories Office**
Tel: 2852 4801 Fax: 2541 5290	Tel: 2755 4835 Fax: 2796 0369	Tel: 2417 6190 Fax: 2499 3713

Info source: Labour Department Website

中文索引 Chinese Index

英文字母

一畫

二畫

三畫

四畫

五畫

六畫

七畫

八畫

九畫

十畫

十一畫

十二畫

十三畫

十四畫

十五畫

十六畫

十七畫

十八畫

十九畫

二十一畫

二十五畫

英文索引 English Index

Numbers

A

B

C

D

E

F

G

H

T

U

V

W

X

Y

出版 Publisher

香港聾人福利促進會手語中心
The Hong Kong Society for the Deaf
Sign Language Centre

香港灣仔軒尼詩道15號溫莎公爵社會服務大廈903室
Rm 903, Duke of Windsor Social Service Building, 15 Hennessy Road, Wanchai, H.K.
電話 Tel: (852) 2527-8969 | 傳真 Fax: (852) 2529-3316
電郵 Email: sign@deaf.org.hk | 網址 Website: http://www.deaf.org.hk